60 POSTCARDS

When Rachael lost her mother to cancer, her world was shattered. Deciding to leave notes all over a city in memory of her mum, to mark what would have been her sixtieth birthday, she hand-wrote sixty postcards, each with her email address at the bottom asking the finders to get in touch with their own stories. But one question remained: where should she go? Knowing how much her mum had longed to visit Paris, Rachael set off to France with a group of friends to scatter her memories. Then, after her return home, the emails started flowing in . . .

This one's for you, Mum.
With all of the love that you could imagine,
Paul, Sarah, Hannah and Rachael xxx

'Life isn't about waiting for the storm to pass. It's about learning how to dance in the rain . . . '

Vivian Greene

Contents

Before you start this book, please buy a blank postcard to use as a bookmark.

1

Le Voyage

It was 6.20am on a bitterly crisp December morning. December 6th, 2012, to be precise. And, if I'm honest, I didn't exactly look as classy as I had hoped for the journey ahead. In fact, my puffy eyes and make-up-less face were not a sight that anyone would want to see at any hour of day, let alone at *that* time. *This is way too early for me!* The brisk winter morning was a very severe wake-up call, which was going to be helpful as we were running a little late. *An occurrence I am definitely used to, I'm afraid.* We were scuttling down Regent's Canal from my house to King's Cross St Pancras as quickly as our sleepy bodies could carry us. It is just a stone's throw away but it seemed like a million miles on that morning. Hurrying along with me were Katie, one of my housemates, and my school friend Beth, who had travelled up from Exeter the evening before. We rushed through the station, over-sized bags in tow. One bag was taking a lot longer than the others to drag along. Katie's suitcase was broken and we couldn't help but laugh at her lagging behind. *Of all the suitcases to bring!* I was calling another school friend as we ran. Bethan (*two people with 'Beth' at the beginning of their name — I know, this could get confusing*) must still be on the tube — I got her voicemail. No problem, we would meet her there. As we walked through the entrance to the station, we spotted her and we all embraced, hugging as if we hadn't seen each other for years. (It had only been a matter of weeks, but this time was different! This was special.)

Oh, the sleepiness was over and we were now wide-awake and raring to go. Reality was kicking in. This was it — journey time! Tickets — check. Passport — check. Pants — check. We were ready to board the Eurostar. Destination — Paris.

By the time we'd passed through security and were boarding the train, the excitement level had risen even further; our 'outdoor' voices were in full force. I can only imagine the fear of fellow passengers, 'Oh, please tell me those girls are not sitting near us.' I mean — I can only imagine it *now*. I definitely couldn't at the time — I flew through the aisle to find my seat number, a shadow of my former (sleepy) self. Bethan and I had booked seats next to each other but Katie and Beth had separate seats in coaches miles away. They decided to take a chance and took the two empty seats behind us assuming, understandably, that they would be kicked out when the rightful owners arrived. But amazingly, as the train departed no one came. You may think 'amazingly' is a bit strong. It does sound a little dramatic, I grant you. But, you see, it was a full carriage. Every single seat was taken. Every one! Apart from the two Katie and Beth were in. A stroke of luck! And it turns out that it was not the first bit of luck that we would experience on this trip.

We took it in turns to hit the buffet carriage (no offence to Katie's pre-made picnic snacks) to stock up on breakfast croissants. We were preparing our stomachs for the dietary delights that would be devoured on the weekend ahead. It dawned on me at the time how like a school trip it was — being on a train to somewhere fun, being over-excited and nattering away with your best mates. Except this time we were adults (supposedly) and we were allowed to drink alcohol — even better.

It may have been first thing in the morning but, naturally, not long into the journey we cracked open a bottle of Champagne. Sorry, did I say Champagne? It was probably cava, come to think of it. (*I would just like to point out that drinking at 7.30am is not a habit of mine.*) We made the unanimous decision that pretty much the only time you can get away with sipping morning bubbles is on the way to Paris. Especially on your first ever visit to the city, which it was mine. Keeping our British roots close to us, we poured the bubbly into none other than 'Keep calm and keep drinking' red cups. *Pure class.* It was celebration time — we were going there for someone's birthday. But, not only that, we were on a mission. This was no ordinary city break.

In true school-trip style, we spent the journey laughing, joking and turning around in our seats. The people in seats 21a and 22b were probably wondering what the fuss was about. *If only you knew!* I had celebrated my own birthday on the previous weekend and the build-up to this trip had been huge — mainly because it just meant so much to me. Before we had even finished our croissants and our glasses of fizz (which I was no longer sipping, as such), we were through the tunnel and looking out at the French countryside. *Bonjour!* The phone network soon changed to *L'Orange* (or something similar) and we said farewell to our Wi-Fi, with a wave to the far-too-overused Facebook

4

and Twitter. Now that *certainly* wasn't an issue in my school days — I don't think I even owned a mobile phone until I was about fifteen years old. Ah, the days where you had to call someone's landline to speak to them or even arrange a time and a place to meet in advance and hope for the best!

After a read of our books, a little practise of our *français* and after I had, so kindly, finished off the rest of the bottle (*hiccup*), we pulled into the *Gare du Nord dans Paris* (insert French accent here). I realised as I stood up that it was not only excitement that I was dizzy with. We hopped (I stumbled) off the train and, for some reason, I thought that this would be a great opportunity for me to stop in my tracks and take a picture of the Eurostar logo on the side of the train. This would have been a good time to take the shot, if it weren't for all the other people piling off the train. I gave up pretty quickly and the girls reassured me, in a very cheeky manner, that it probably wouldn't be the last chance I would get to take a photo of the Eurostar logo, given that I resided in King's Cross. *Good point.* And so, I put the camera away for now.

We queued for a taxi outside the station. I was preparing to use my (terrible) French but, of course, as I got into the car I decided it would be easier to show them the address written on a piece of paper. *What a cop-out.* We were heading east to an apartment in Montmartre, near La Fourche Métro. I gazed out of the window in awe at the streets of the Parisian world that I had been longing to see for as long as I could remember. How I got to the age of twenty-eight — living in King's Cross for the past two — without visiting The City of Light was an absolute scandal. I had only seen it from afar, though — in films, in my dreams and from conversations with friends who had been. *I'm finally here!*

It was strange to be so head-over-heels in love — so passionate — about a city that I had never even seen with my own eyes. My fascination with the French language was partly responsible, despite only having a B in GCSE French under my belt. I have always been keen to learn it properly. Add it to my list entitled, 'I'll-get-around-to-it-next-year' — a list that is forever growing, with very few lines being crossed off. *I'll get around to it next year. Hopefully.*

Rolling up to the private cobbled street (just as the Airbnb description had informed us), I gave the host, Madame Antoinette, a call. She came out to greet us and led us to the apartment that we would be staying in for the next three nights. She was as stylish and as elegant as could be and so friendly and welcoming that within a matter of minutes it was as if we had known her for years. I liked her immediately. Now, if you are an Airbnb fan like myself, you will recognise that anxious feeling as you pass through the front door of your temporary accommodation — especially if you have been the person responsible for booking it. *Will it look like the pictures? Will everyone resent me for the whole weekend if it doesn't?* Well, as I entered Antoinette's house on that morning, I couldn't help but gawp in amazement, 'oohing and aahing' out loud at the sight before me. It was even better than it had looked on the screen. It was pretty, Parisian and simply perfect.

This 'multi-level loft' (as Antoinette calls it) was a treat for the eye — a fascinating mixture between modern and antique. I felt like I was walking into a film set (*the camera men must be on a break!*). The kitchen area was on the right as soon as you walked through the front door — above it on the top shelf a selection of the host's designer handbags stood neatly in a row. *Parisiennes know how to shop!* The downstairs space was huge and divided into three different living spaces. There was a dining area with a large wooden table and chairs — perfect for the dinners we would have together. The lounge area at the front of the house was kitted out with leather sofas, a wicker chair and grand paintings on both walls. The main event was a further lounge area — steps led down to a U-shaped, cushioned seating area, topped off with a hanging light, low in the centre. This space was known as the 'oriental lounge' to Antoinette but it soon became 'the sunken area' to us and then, later, 'the best sunken area of my life'. (I mean, we hadn't exactly come across any others, but we very much doubted that we would find one that could top this delight.)

The decor was quirky but cool. A big shelf filled with all kinds of books covered a wall with fairy lights draped all over. (*I may be in my late twenties but, hey, I still adore fairy lights.*) The most bizarre (albeit interesting) feature of the room was a lectern. *Random!* An erotic picture hung above it which provided a giggle or two, being the mature adults that we are. A small white staircase with slightly loose (which added to the fun) metal banisters led up to a mezzanine set out as a study. From here there were spiral stairs taking you to the next level. I wandered around endless bedrooms, trying to figure out which one to shotgun for myself. There was even a secret room at the very top, which you took a ladder up to enter. *Too much effort, especially after a tipple or two — I'll leave that one for someone else!* The whole place was so unusual and beautiful — I was more than pleased that this apartment would be our home for the weekend. I wanted to move in permanently. *Maybe I should lose my passport?* My first trip to Paris was already falling into place perfectly.

Antoinette gave us the lowdown about how to use everything in the house, offered tips on the local shops and restaurants and then handed over the keys. *They are mine now!* Off she went. She would be staying in her studio just a few doors down in case we needed her. And with that knowledge we made a note to ourselves — be on your best behaviour when coming home at night. *'Outdoor' voices will not be welcome.* After claiming our bedrooms, Beth, Bethan, Katie and I headed out to suss out the local area. We found a lovely little café for lunch. On such a freezing morning it was not only the menu that drew us in, but also the glowing light of the heaters that hung above the tables. *This would do nicely.* We went in and took our seats and made ourselves comfort-able. While we were choosing what to order, the heaters were switched off and we were shivering once again. The waiters explained that it was too expensive to keep them on. *It's so cold — we will tip more!* We made our shivers more dramatic, chattering teeth and everything. It worked — they rolled their eyes, smiled at us and reluctantly clicked them back on. *Winner.*

It was at this point that I started to lag — the early morning was catching up with me. There was only one thing for it — it was time for our first glass of *vin rouge*. My first glass of wine for my first time in Paris and I had three of my best friends in the world to share it with. *Fantastique.*

The glass of red warmed me up a treat. We wandered back from the café passing a gorgeous jewellery shop for a quick browse. We went to the nearby *supermarché* to stock up on food and drink for the evening, and then we were back in our new home and ready for more people to arrive. Yes there were more to come. *So many more.*

We had a few hours to spare before the first of the troops were to hit the apartment, so we made ourselves a pot of fresh coffee and settled down in the 'best sunken area of our lives'. We all relaxed in our humble abode, feeling like we owned the place. The rest of the gang were going to be filtering into the apartment during the evening. We had got the table ready with nibbles and drinks, the fairy lights had been switched on and we were prepared for our first evening of fun in the apartment of dreams. As everyone else grabbed their books, I reached into my bag for something else — a stack of postcards. A bit premature to be writing postcards a few hours into the trip, you may think? But I did tell you that this was no ordinary city break — far from it! Not only was I there to sightsee and spend quality time with my closest friends, but I was also there on a mission — a mission that involved not one, not two, but 60 postcards. I began to write my message, postcard after postcard but it was only half an hour later when I had to put them to one side to greet someone at the door.

The first arrival was my housemate from home, Trent. No stranger to Paris, Trent had found the hidden gem of an apartment without any trouble at all. As soon as he came in, he dropped his bag and headed straight for the comfort of our favourite seating area, filling us in on his day in London. Working for a music channel, he always had great stories about the latest acts and celebrities on his interview list and I was always gagging to hear all about it. *How the other half live.*

The next knock on our door came an hour or so later, from two more group members

— it was Clare and David who had arrived straight from school. *Not children themselves — they teach the youngens.* The poor duo were completely soaked through and looked like they needed a good cheering up. Thankfully we had our table full of yummy delights. *That should do the trick.*

As we listened to music, and everyone chatted and laughed — some getting introduced to each other for the very first time — my third London housemate Beccy flew through the door. She was feeling giddy after spending the evening in London working at the Women in Film and Television Awards. We laughed with her as she told us how emotional it was and how she couldn't help but have teary eyes at every single award. She said she had felt so glamorous telling everyone as she was leaving the event that she was off to catch the Eurostar to Paris. She then announced excitedly, 'One day, I'll be sat at one of those tables, not setting them!' *I know Beccy — I have no doubt that it will happen for her.*

My friends Stewart and Amy were the last to join the fold — and it sounded like it had been quite the journey for them both. Stewart is one of the best story-tellers I know and we all huddled round to hear what was bound to be a cracker. He had dashed to Heathrow in a last-minute sprint to catch the evening Air France flight to Charles De Gaulle. He told us that instead of enjoying our company, he had been lumbered next to a group of extremely loud Liverpudlian school children who were visiting on a French exchange. Luckily he had a gin and tonic (*or two I suspect!*) and some mini pretzels to keep him going. *Thank goodness for in-flight refreshments.*

Amy had been travelling on the Eurostar at the very same time that Stewart was in the air, in a similar last-minute fashion. *These are people after my own heart.* Neither Amy nor Stewart had a clue where the apartment was and thankfully had managed to meet in order to find their way together. Well, it turns out they ended up getting lost together as they asked many a bemused passer-by — *Où est le 'secret cobbled street'?*

As we all gathered around the sunken area, I felt content. My best friends, with a couple more on the way, had made such an effort to attend this very important weekend. When I told you that we were there to celebrate someone's birthday, what I neglected to explain was that it was not the birthday of anyone on the trip. It was for my mother's sixtieth birthday. In memory of what *would* have been her sixtieth birthday. Because my wonderful mum had passed away very suddenly from cancer in February earlier that year.

As I said — this would be no ordinary city break.

We were on a mission of remembrance.

2

Never Forget

As I stood outside the gigantic Topshop on Oxford Street eagerly awaiting its opening — hoping to dash in and out as quickly as possible to grab a last-minute outfit and escape the bombardment of tourists that would inevitably fill the streets and shops at any moment — I felt my phone vibrate in my pocket. 'Sarah' flashed on the screen. I thought it was a little strange that one of my younger sisters was calling me at such an early hour. It wasn't early by most people's standards but she knew all too well that I was usually in bed at this time on a Saturday morning. I presumed the call must be about my house party that evening, which both my sisters were coming up to London for. I answered the phone with excitement but Sarah had a very calm tone to her voice — the kind of calm where it becomes evident very quickly that this was most definitely not a party call. Something was wrong. Sarah explained, never wavering from that tone, that

Mum had suffered an attack of excruciating abdominal pains. My heart dropped and I felt a rush of panic flow through my whole body. *What the hell is going on?*

Sarah explained that Mum had refused to get an ambulance but agreed that our family friend and doctor, Andy, could come over to the house to help. Andy had provided Mum with some pain relief and insisted that she should, and would, go straight to see her local GP at the beginning of the week. It was too difficult to tell at this stage what was wrong but the first thoughts were that it could well be gallstones. *Yes — gallstones — that must be it.* Right, so she would be tested as soon as possible, they could take the stones out and the problem would be solved — sorted. I said that I would come home straight away but Sarah assured me that Mum was feeling much better and had been adamant that both Sarah and my youngest sister, Hannah, were to come up to mine for the night, just as we had planned. I wasn't sure about it at all but we agreed to Mum's wishes.

As I got off the phone, I broke down in the street, frozen to the spot in which I stood — shoppers whizzing by me too busy to notice. London can be like that — you really are a pin in the needle stack. You can stand on the busiest street in the city and feel like no one even knows you are there. In that moment, I really felt just one of the 8.2 million population — I was completely alone. I wanted to scream but instead I wiped my tears and walked into the shop, trying to make sense of what I had just heard. *I can't believe it.*

Sarah had told me time and time again throughout the call that everything had settled down at home now — Mum was fine, she was feeling OK. *Why am I still so worried?* What was getting to me was the fact that my mum did not get ill. Not ever. I couldn't even remember a time in the past 20 years when she had even needed a doctor's appointment. Just like most mums, she was ridiculously resilient and would crack on no matter what. She even refused to take paracetamol with a headache, for crying out loud. *Not even on a hangover.* If I am honest with myself, I had a deeply sad feeling that this may be something more serious. Warning bells were ringing at the back of my head. But I tried to block the ringing out. *Ignore it.* Everything would be OK. We really thought that everything would be OK.

My mind flashed back to my actual birthday, just three days earlier. I assumed it would be a family-less affair with my parents and two sisters living in Dorset and unable to take time off work. But, due to a last-minute teachers' strike, my mum came up to London to spend the day with me. I met her at Victoria Station and I gave her a big hug — I was so excited to see her. I linked my arm through hers, as I did whenever I saw her, and led the way to the next floor to grab a coffee to kick-start the day. But as we were sitting drinking our coffees, she seemed completely distracted. She had a cheeky look on her face and a twinkle in her eye. *What is she up to? Why does she keep looking around?* It seemed like I was missing something. Turns out that I was — my sister Hannah. We all burst into fits of giggles as Hannah explained that she had been walking past the table continually for about five minutes before I had noticed. I began to cry into my coffee cup with joy. *Not a great birthday look.*

Mum presented me with a card and some lovely little gifts — as always. I don't know about you but my family pester me for a birthday/Christmas list every year. I suppose it makes sense for you to receive what you actually want. But, oh, indecisive-me was just so, well, indecisive that I never got round to it. I like a good surprise (note my ridiculous reaction to Hannah's appearance). I always figured that Mum knew me so well that she would always get it right. And she did — she always delivered. This year was a little different, though. Mum was all too aware, through several of my ramblings, that there was somewhere I was desperate to visit — Paris, The City of Love.

As I opened the birthday card from my family, I was delighted to find that I had received vouchers for the Eurostar. This would *finally* kick-start me into action — I would get to Paris at last!

After the coffee stop and the appearance of my surprise guest, we were off in a taxi to the Southbank. This is the place in London that will remind me most of my times spent with Mum on her trips up to see me — so many of our meetings were spent there, wandering, drinking, eating, visiting the Tate or Somerset House across the river and generally soaking up the London vibe.

As we pottered around the stalls along the Thames we embraced the seasonal atmosphere; Christmassy decorations and tunes played out along the riverbank. The smell of roast chestnuts and mulled wine filled the air. It was heavenly festive. Hannah found an unusual stall and picked up a wooden tie to buy Dad as part of his Christmas present. The most worrying part about this was just how much he loved it. (*They have wooden bow ties as well — he'd like one of those, too,* no *doubt. Oh dear.*) Meanwhile, Mum was drawn to a photography stall just across the other side. She bought four photos of images depicting letters spelling out the word 'LOVE', her family name. I adore that picture. *I adore that name, too.*

We wandered along, street entertainers performing for the bustling crowds. Much to Mum and Hannah's amusement, I was approached by a man who insisted that he put a bracelet on my arm. *So kind.* I soon realised this was not a gift and we scrambled about for some change. *So expensive.*

By the time we had browsed the stalls and Hannah and Mum had made their purchases (along with having a good laugh at bracelet-gate), it was time to grab something to eat — we hit a pizza place for lunch. As we reached the end of the meal, it was clear that Mum's appetite was not all there. She had barely touched her food. 'I'm OK — I think I may have a tummy bug,' she told us. How I wish that was all it had been.

My day of birthday fun came to an end as Mum and Hannah needed to get back to Dorset, ready for work the next day, and I had plans to meet friends for drinks in Angel. Time had flown far too quickly. I felt sad when they left me that day. I was always sad to say goodbye, whether it was my family leaving me or me leaving them. I consider myself a real 'home girl'. I was lucky; Dorset (Merley, Wimborne, to be precise) was close enough for me to pop back for frequent weekend visits and I did so once a month — it was just over two hours on a train. *Waterloo to Poole* — easy.

As they left me, I was so glad that the teachers' strike had fallen on my birthday and that Mum could be with me. I felt incredibly lucky, and even more so now. I had no idea that it would be the last birthday that I would get to spend with my mother.

After the phone call from Sarah, I grabbed a dress in Topshop but my mind was still whirling from the news that she had delivered. I decided to get some fresh air and walk back to mine, taking my time. When I returned home, I found Katie in the kitchen and told her what had happened. She sensed my panic and talked it through with me as we started to get the house ready for the party that evening.

I called home twice that day so that I could speak to Mum — Dad said that she was resting and wasn't able to talk. I usually spoke to Mum on the phone every other day — on my walk home from work, just after she had spoken to Hannah on her walk from her work to the car. We had a routine. I wanted desperately to hear her voice — even just for a moment. But Dad kept telling me that she couldn't — she needed to rest. This had never happened before and it was driving me insane. *Please call me, Mum.*

The house party was obviously not the fun event I had planned. My mind was on Mum. I felt so distracted, worrying about her and wishing that I had just gone home to Dorset. But Mum would have hated that — she hated a fuss being made about her. I spent a lot of time hiding in my room that evening and I remember at one point sitting on the steps outside with my friend Beth telling her that even though everyone was saying that Mum was fine, I was not buying it, not for a second. I cried me a river and then continued to drink far too much mulled wine, which never helps. *The room is spinning.*

I went home the next weekend to see her. She had lost a little weight since my birthday. The test for gallstones had come back negative so that one had been ruled out. Mum seemed convinced that it was some kind of digestive infection and she said that she was feeling OK and was sure she would be on the mend soon. She almost convinced me. That was until I questioned her a little more on the symptoms that she had. She told me and I asked her if that was it — if there was anything else at all. I knew my mum too well — I could tell by the look on her face that there were things that she was choosing not to tell me. I wondered if it was because she didn't want to admit it to herself, or whether she was trying to protect me and my sisters. Because I had done something that you should never do — I had gone on to Google to do my own research on hearing that we still didn't have a diagnosis. Well, that really was a bad idea. As you can imagine, it came up with all of my worst nightmares. Still, I had to believe Mum when she said that she was not feeling too bad. We would wait for the next set of tests, including a colonoscopy that was booked for January. Why it had to wait so long I wasn't sure but she didn't want to go private. *I wish now that I had pushed for that.*

After a couple of weeks of working in London as usual, it was time for me to head back home to Dorset for the Christmas holidays. I had worked through Mum's birthday, knowing that I would see her just the next week. *Yet another regret of mine. Why am I so stupid?* When I got back I noticed that she had lost even more weight and the colour in her cheeks had faded dramatically. Still, stubbornly, she was adamant that she was doing OK. Nicola, my

23

cousin, was down to stay with us along with her two daughters, Amber and Lucy. Nicola was the daughter of my mum's sister Veronica, who had died of cancer when we were little, and we had become closer and closer to them over the years. We loved having them with us. As the girls were a bit younger, it kept the Christmas spirit even more alive. And it also made sure we were up early on Christmas morning (even though they would have to scream up to me several times before I was able to rise, recovering as I often was from a Christmas Eve drinking session in the local village). 'Don't ruin your dinner,' Mum would warn me. *Pass me some paracetamol and I will be good to go (maybe!)*.

It was Christmas as usual, well almost. With Mum just a little weaker and paler than usual, Sarah and I had offered to take over the Christmas lunch duties. When I say that, what I actually mean is that Sarah was Head Chef and I was Sous Chef — or 'Official Veg Chopper', more like. Sarah has a comedy Ramsey-esque approach to cooking, which part terrified me and part left me in stitches. *How wrong can you go chopping carrots? Very wrong — apparently*. Hannah, being the cheeky girl that she is, kept poking her head around the kitchen door and asking if she could help at all. Before either Sarah or I could answer, she would shout, 'Looks fine to me!' and *vamoosh* — she was out of the door and out of sight!

After lunch had been devoured (*a good effort by us, I must say — especially the carrots*), we were heading for the lounge to undo the top buttons of our jeans and chill by the fire with a film on the box. Once our dinner had gone down, the Wii was set up and it was time for some karaoke. Mum got involved and it was slightly bizarre but mostly hilarious to hear her rendition of 'Don't Cha' by the Pussycat Dolls. *I never thought I would see the day.* We played Articulate, which was always a laugh. I can't handle the pressure of that game — I am terrible, which is odd considering there is usually no shutting me up! Bubble and squeak was Dad's speciality for dinner and, with all of the games and overeating, it was time for an early night.

The rest of the Christmas holiday was very chilled and I enjoyed two wonderful moments of bonding with Mum. The first was when we went to Hobbycraft, the local craft store, to pick up some bits and bobs for invitations that I was making for an event later that year. Mum and I had gone to the café there for lunch after we had everything I needed. We shared a sandwich and I noticed she barely touched hers, but she seemed on very good form. Before long we were engrossed in a deep and meaningful. We were talking about relationships and I suddenly realised I had never actually quizzed her about how she had been certain that Dad was the one for her. I'm a rom-com-watching, fairytale-ending believer, but Mum told me that it hadn't been like that at all. The dramatic music cut out in my head. She had dated a few fellas before Dad, who she thought she had fallen hopelessly in love with. But with Dad, she explained, she just 'knew'. It was as simple as that. The music began to play in my head once more.

The second moment was when Mum and I had the lounge to ourselves. Ever since I got home for Christmas, I had been keen to show Mum a DVD that I knew she would love. It was Take That's *Progress* concert. Take That were my favourite band when I was little. I wasn't an obsessive fan — I mean, I was disappointed when they broke up but I didn't cry. *Heartless, I know!* (Unlike a friend of mine who confesses that she was sent home from her Spanish lesson in hysterics and spent the rest of the day making a shrine with candles followed by a poem made up of their song lyrics. *Wow. Just wow.*) I had all of their albums, videos and I even had stickers up in my room (which ended up sticking to the walls for far longer than I intended, forgetting how difficult it is to take them off!). Poor Mum had been subjected to years of Take That videos. Imagine my delight when the band reunited in later years and Mum became a fan, too. She had a soft spot for Gary Barlow, naturally, 'Ooh, isn't he lovely!' *Calm down, love!* We settled down to watch the concert from our armchairs. Before long we were joining in and it was when we were singing along to Pray that I noticed Mum crying. I laughed at her and asked if it was because I was twenty-eight years old and I was still sitting in the lounge with my mum watching Take That. *Some things never change.* She laughed with me, wiped her tears and we continued watching, throwing our hands up in the air to 'Never Forget' and giving a standing ovation and a cheer at the end. I knew she'd love it. It was such a wonderful moment that I knew I would never forget (pun completely intended).

Because the DVD had gone down so well, I couldn't resist buying her a copy and sneaking it into the glove compartment of her car when she was dropping me at the coach station for my journey back up to London. I boarded the coach smiling and waving but as I sat down on my seat my face went blank. *I can't smile anymore*. I had been in denial over Christmas. Looking back at Mum in the moment that I said goodbye, I realised she looked seriously ill.

3

Sixteen Days

New Year was celebrated (reluctantly) and the year of 2012 had begun for most people — but not for us. By the third week of January I was trying to continue London life, being sure to call Mum as much as possible but we were *still* waiting — for an agonisingly long time — to find out what was wrong with her. *This is getting ridiculous.*

What followed were three phone calls that changed our world forever.

Thursday 26th January, 2012 — The first phone call

It was early afternoon and I was slumped at my desk at work. My productivity levels were at an all-time low and I spent most of the day staring at the screen on my phone. If I wasn't doing that, then I was just staring into space — going through in my head all of the different conversations that I could possibly have with Mum about the results of her colonoscopy that she was having that morning. My phone flashed and I leapt up — it was Dad. Leaving my computer screens completely open for everyone to see, I dashed out to the hallway — close enough for me to be able to pick up the phone quickly, far enough away to be out of earshot of my colleagues. I already knew which one of the conversations I would be having. It was Dad calling me, not Mum. *That says it all.*

'It's not good, I'm afraid, Rach — it's cancer.'

That 'c' word echoed around in my head. They had found a large tumour in her stomach. *No. Please, no.*

It is so difficult to explain in words how I felt at this point. I was hearing the news that, deep down, I had been half-expecting. But that ton of bricks hit me just as hard as if it were coming out of nowhere. I tried with all of my might, with every part of me, to keep calm and keep it together on the phone for my dad. Well, and for me. *Someone help us.*

It was only when I pressed 'end call' that I noticed how much I was shaking. The tears were on their way and in danger of flowing at any moment. I had to get out of there quickly. I ran to my desk, pressed 'save' on every document at the speed of light and then grabbed my bag, muttering to my colleagues that I had to leave. I caught my boss, Rob's, eye and didn't even need to ask him if I could have a word — he followed me out to the very spot that I had received the news. His whole body sank as I told him. Working at the company for almost three years, he (and most of my colleagues) knew when I was not myself. I had expressed my concern — my fear — that something was seriously wrong with Mum. 'Just go,' he said with a nod, reassuring me that I should forget about work and do whatever I needed to do back home. For the company that I worked for — family came first every time.

Before I left the building, I wanted to see my closest friends there — Caroline, Cat and Marcus — to let them know what was going on. First stop was Marcus's desk. He worked on the same floor as me and, after meeting in my first month with the company, we had become close friends. We have similar senses of humour and have had a very supportive friendship ever since. I rushed over to his desk to find that it was empty. 'Where is he?' I asked his colleague, struggling to hide the panic on my face. It turned out that he was in an internal meeting and was, thankfully, able to slip out to see me. I met him in a meeting room and I finally let the tears flow properly as we hugged in silence. After words of support and a promise to come and meet me after work, I left Marcus and met Cat and Caroline downstairs. I cried again, as they did with me, and then I went off for a long walk. I needed to be alone — at least I thought so. I didn't make it far until I stopped at a café. I collapsed on a seat — the phone conversation was going over and over in my head.

I spoke to my dad again and, between us, we decided that it would be best if I came home the next morning. If I left straight away, I wouldn't make it back in time before Mum was in bed and leaving it till the next day would give me time to calm myself down and see her when the initial shock had passed. I knew my dad so well — he didn't have to say as much but there had clearly been an unspoken rule made at this point — there would be as little fuss or drama around Mum as possible. A family rule had been written and it was one that I was determined to do my best to adhere to.

Caroline and Marcus met me for dinner and were both amazing at distracting me or listening as and when I needed. They psyched me up and told me that I could be strong. My game face was on.

★ ★ ★

As I walked into the lounge to see Mum for the first time after hearing the news, I remembered the support of my friends and, of course, my conversation with Dad. I decided that, rather than being miserable, I would try to make light of it all. I may have gone a little far as I was so nervous. I announced to Mum that I heard she was being a drama queen (*still makes me cringe*) but she laughed and I gave her a big bear hug. There was not much that we could do at this point apart from wait until the next week when the oncologists were to investigate further and look at potential treatment options. *Why can't we find out right now?*

I wanted to catch my dad on his own so, once I had spent some time with Mum, putting on the happy front as I had promised myself, I managed to catch him in the kitchen. I told him that I understood that both he and Mum would, understandably, want to protect us, but that my way of dealing with this was by knowing all of the facts. I did not want to be in the dark about any single detail. I knew that neither Sarah nor Hannah had asked for this and so I understood I was to keep things to myself. Dad assured me that he would be completely honest. But what he told me next came as a complete shock. He told me that the results of Mum's scans had shown shadows on the liver. There was a chance that the cancer had already spread. I couldn't believe what I was hearing. *Mum!* If this was the case, then why did we have to wait a whole WEEK to hear what the next step was? *This doesn't make sense.* I tried to keep my cool. *I can feel the anger rising.*

As I came away from that conversation I realised that I was so wrapped up in the world of what was happening to 'my mum', I had neglected to spare a thought for my poor dad. Dad's job is headteacher of a large middle school in Dorset and I realised that his professional manner was transferring into home life. He was so composed and holding everything together. He had been in constant communication with me, which I hadn't even appreciated fully until that moment. He was having to deal with everything, all at once. *This is his wife — I need to remember that.*

Now, guess what I did next? I went on Google again. If this was, potentially, stage four cancer then all I could find on every single site that I searched was a prognosis of five years. I had only just found out that my mother had cancer — this was all too much. Panic set in. *I'm beginning to swear a lot.* And poor Mum, the pain was increasing every single day for her — how was she going to handle the mental strain of what she was about to face? I told myself to stay strong but I didn't know how long I was going to be able to cope for. I wondered when my breaking point would come. *It feels like when, not if.*

I stayed at home for a few days, spending time with Mum but making sure not to mention what was happening. As I watched Hannah brushing Mum's hair one morning, I realised that this was a complete role reversal. Mum had brushed our hair every day when we were little, and now we were doing it for her — she was becoming too weak to do it for herself. *She is so young — this shouldn't be happening so soon.*

There was a moment when Hannah and I were sitting in the front room with her and in a conversation about what we could have for tea, Mum said 'Heenz beanz' instead of 'Heinz Beans'. In any normal situation we would have all laughed hysterically at the mishap. But as Hannah and I were laughing away I realised that there was no sound coming from Mum's side of the room. Her face was blank and she looked in serious pain. She couldn't laugh and it broke my heart into pieces.

★ ★ ★

I went back up to London to head into the office the following week. While continuing with work, I also wanted to speak to HR about the situation. All I could tell them was that I had no idea what was going to happen and that we were waiting for more news from the oncologists. HR were very understanding and they assured me that I would be supported with each step as and when it happened. *This will all be settled soon, I'm sure.* I tried to carry on as normal but normal was beginning to slip away from my grasp. I was waiting for the next bit of news. And when that came, it wasn't good at all.

On my third evening back in London I heard from Dad. Mum's body temperature was racing from one extreme to the other — she was freezing in one moment and boiling in the next — and the discomfort she was suffering was becoming all too much. The tumour in her stomach was making it increasingly difficult to eat — solids were out of the question and even liquids were tough for her to swallow. The only thing that she seemed to be able to enjoy was POLO mints. *I will never eat those again.* Without being able to swallow anything at all, it was clear that she needed help and she needed it quickly. After Andy, the GP, had visited the house, he decided the best thing was to get an ambulance so that Mum could be taken straight in to hospital and could be seen as quickly as possible. She was taken to the Ansty Ward at first and then to Ward B4. I had no clue what these meant until Sarah explained that the first was an assessment ward and the second was a colorectal one. *Somebody has to help her.* She was staying overnight. *Mum will hate that.*

After her first night in the ward, Mum was told that she would be going in for further scans to check on the shadows that had been spotted on her liver. One of the nurses looking after Mum was, purely by chance, one of Sarah's best friends Claire. This was brilliant news. We all know how cold and desperately miserable hospitals can be and with my dad and sisters only able to visit at limited times, Mum at least had a familiar face around her. She had also told us how fond she was of the specialist nurse, Caroline. I was so relieved to hear that she was in good hands. She was given a drip to rehydrate her and to get her back on track.

In she went for her scans and the results that came back were extremely odd but showed a sign of hope. The family seemed to be in high spirits. I was at work when I received the news that the doctors had come to the conclusion that whatever it was on Mum's liver had grown so much in just one week that it didn't seem possible it was cancer — it couldn't have developed that quickly. She would stay overnight again and then they would run tests the next day to check for fluids because it was highly likely that it was cysts. *Right, OK.*

I had been at work when I received the positive messages from the family about the latest updates. I found Marcus and we went off on our daily lunchtime walk around the block behind Oxford Street. He could tell something was up. There was. I told him that what I had just heard was either the best news we could wish for or the absolute worst. Because I knew all too well that if it wasn't cysts then this was going to be more horrendous than any one of us could ever have imagined. Especially if they had not seen anything grow that quickly before. *I shuddered at the thought.* Marcus listened, he took it all in and let me get everything out in the open as I ranted away, quite calmly, trying once again to prepare my heart and my head for every possible situation. I knew that I was going to have a sleepless night ahead and my bag was going to be packed and ready for my next trip home.

Friday 3rd February, 2012 — The second phone call

The next morning we all received a text from Mum sent from her hospital bed:

> Morning all. Quite a good night and OK this morning. Only managed half of Corrie last night so will catch up this morning. Will let you know when I hear the game plan for the day. But don't forget, it's a waiting game. Van the man is on — Have I told you lately? Well I hope I have. xx

That was one of Mum and Dad's favourite songs. The text message brought a tear to my eye. It was amazing to hear Mum sounding so chirpy, especially as she had just endured night two in her horrifically clinical accommodation all by herself. With such a light-hearted message I began to believe that things might be looking up after all.

I had just finished my day at work and was heading out of the building, on my way to the local pub for a drink, when I saw the familiar sight of 'Dad' flashing on my phone. It must be news on the cysts. I picked up the phone and Dad got straight to the point. It wasn't cysts. I remember saying the 'F' word. I remember falling back against a wall to lean on. I remember feeling like I was going to throw up as he said, 'It's too late for treatment, I'm afraid — there is nothing they can do for Mum.'

Why not? They must be able to do *something*. Can't they at least try? I reverted back to being a child. *I want my mummy. Please, don't take her away from me. Please.*

Her cancer was breaking all sorts of records; unrecognisably aggressive even to the specialists treating her. Sorry, not treating her — assessing her. Treatment was not an option, apparently. *How can everyone sit back and do NOTHING?*

All of my feelings on hearing the news had been utterly selfish at first. I couldn't live without my mum. *I won't.* It was all too sudden. *We only found out she had cancer a week ago.* And then, as I put the phone down and I thought about how my mum must be feeling, it killed me inside. *She knows she is going to die.* I wished that I could erase her memory right there and then. I started shivering in shock, still leaning against the wall I had slumped against on receiving the worst news I had ever heard in my life.

I walked straight into the pub and I ignored every person who tried to talk to me. I didn't care — I had no energy to respond to them. I just needed to find Caroline and Marcus.

When I did, I asked them to meet me outside straight away. I sat on the bench outside the door still shaking all over and they walked up to me with worried faces. I told them the news and broke down as they both held me. Silence again. None of us could speak. This was it — it was over before we even had a chance to fight it. *My mother is going to die.*

I knew what I had to do was get myself together and travel back home the next day. But getting myself together felt nigh on impossible. I messaged my sisters, called a few of my closest friends and then I decided to have some drinks. *Not advisable but I didn't want to go home.* The only good thing to happen that evening was that there was a warning of a Norovirus outbreak at the hospital and so Mum was going to be discharged and back in the comfort of our home.

I stayed with Caroline and Marcus at the pub for a while and then we went to a Spanish bar to meet my housemates. It was such a strange atmosphere. I didn't know what to do and nor did they. But they stayed with me. They didn't leave my side and I needed that. And then when I finally gave in and went home to bed, I cried for hours. I cried until I had exhausted myself so much I had no choice but to sleep. It was only for a few hours but I needed any sleep I could get to be prepared for the real-life nightmare ahead.

When I got home to Dorset the following morning, I was in such a bad state. I had to do everything possible not to let it show to Mum, though. It had been hard enough getting the news that she had cancer, but now this? I couldn't make any stupid comments about her being a drama queen, that was for sure. *I never should have said that the first time.* I had been gone from home just a matter of days but Mum looked completely grey now. The life was being washed out of her. *She is starting to look less like my mum every time I see her.* Dad told me that it was now a matter of making Mum more comfortable. Well, then, that is what we would do. And with that in mind, roles quickly fell into place in the family house.

Dad, well — where do I start? Our hero. He was a husband, a father, a nurse, a friend, a researcher, a calming influence, a protector, a taxi driver and a messenger — he was everything and more. He has always been a hero in my eyes, but it was at this time that he shone so brightly. I could never be more proud and grateful for his warrior approach at a time when he must have been killing inside. He was losing the love of his life. *How can I ever help him?*

Sarah followed in Mum and Dad's wonderful footsteps and is a teacher. She has inherited so many of Mum's traits. Her role was a nurturing one and she was cooking and cleaning, generally helping around the house. Sarah was the only one of us girls living at home, so she had seen everything. And still, she was being a soldier. She is such a passionate girl and, like me, wears her heart on her sleeve, which is why I was blown away by how she was coping. It made me extremely proud. I was in awe of my little sister who was showing age beyond her years.

Hannah, like myself, chose to go the way of the office for work, and her company was close to where she lived with her partner, Joe. Their house was fifteen minutes from Mum and Dad's, and Hannah was driving over every day to be there at this time. Hannah, the youngest of the family, is a very shy character and likes to hide away at times but, when she is out, she is one of the funniest people I know. She was most definitely burying her head in the sand about what was happening to Mum. It was partly because, at this point, she was completely convinced everything would still be OK. She was using her wit (a definite passing down of the funny gene from Dad) to deflect from the reality of the situation. She had taken on the role of the joker — but what an incredibly important one that was. She kept us laughing, telling jokes and putting on comedy DVDs. A favourite was the Monty Python collection. She even gave her own rendition of John Cleese's Ministry of Silly Walks. She was acting the fool and it was working — she was keeping spirits high and smiles on our faces, including Mum's.

My sisters mean the absolute world to me. We are all so different, yet still so close. I am the eldest with Sarah two years younger than me and Hannah three years younger than her. This is tough to admit, but me? My role? I was the worrier, with anger building up by the second. I was utterly helpless and completely unhelpful. I was concerned that I may be in fear of breaking down. I felt so weak, like there was absolutely nothing I could do. Everyone else was managing so well and I was trying so hard, but nothing was happening. I felt like my body was giving up on me and my heart was breaking — I wasn't mentally strong enough even to think of a way I could help. *I want to run away to a place where my mum is fine and everything is going to be OK.*

I felt guilty because I had not been living down at home. I was thinking the worst about the future. I was panicking for everyone and especially for my sisters. As the eldest, I felt such a responsibility to be there for them. I envisaged already that I would need to become stronger in order to take on a more motherly role. Of course, I knew I would never be Mum but I at least had to try to be more than I had been these past weeks. I had done far too much research and been so intent on Dad telling me every last detail that I suddenly wished that I could take it all away. Sarah knew some of what was happening but Hannah had chosen to be told nothing. I grew increasingly concerned at how different the levels of our knowledge were. All three of us would experience the same pain but the impact was going to be different. It was as if we were falling from different heights. Sarah was on the fifth floor, Hannah was on the roof and I was waiting at the bottom ready to catch them when they fell.

I had been visiting the beach a lot over the past few weeks. It became my place to think or to forget or just to sit watching the waves. I would drive down there and often used it as a time to call Caroline and Marcus — whether it be to cry, talk about Mum or simply talk about nothing. My mum's favourite view in the south was from Evening

Hill overlooking Poole Bay and I had started to visit there, too. I would sit on the bench and look at the view and think about Mum. It was a calming place and I felt like it was my only escape. The only place where I could attempt to clear my head in the slightest.

My dad's sister, Aunty Anne, had come over from Germany to help, which was such a great support. She had been through the same tragic situation when her husband, my Uncle John, had died from bowel cancer. I was so glad that Anne was there, especially for my dad, who was working so hard to do everything right for Mum.

While we were trying to get our head around what was happening, we had a call from the hospital. They were offering a glimmer of hope — Mum was to go in on Monday to see if there was anything at all that they could do. I could tell that Hannah was getting excited by this news but I couldn't see any shimmer in that glimmer.

We took Mum to the hospital on Monday and dropped her and Dad there while Sarah, Hannah and I went to Costa Coffee in Poole town centre to wait until pick-up time. Although I was cynical about this appointment, there was a moment when I wondered if it could be Mum's chance. Maybe Mum would get lucky and be someone who had a miracle recovery. Maybe they could fight this after all? But, just as I was thinking that, I was brought back down to earth as Dad called and said nothing other than to pick them up. Hopes had been dashed once more. *This is insufferable.* This was it — we really were preparing for the end. As we picked them up, my mum was barely recognisable. She came out of the entrance of the hospital in a wheelchair being pushed by my dad. When we arrived home, all that Mum said was that she wanted to be taken to bed. I couldn't even begin to imagine how she must have been feeling. *Why her? Why now? Why MY mother?*

It was decided that rather than taking Mum to a hospice, it would be best for her to be at home — in the family home that she had brought us up in. A bed was going to be delivered for the room next to the conservatory. All I could think was that it was going to be the room that my mother would die in.

The Macmillan nurse came over a couple of days later to see Mum and to talk to us all about the last stages. The girls and I were pulled into a room and I just couldn't believe what was being handed to us. It was leaflets on bereavement counselling. It was a talk on the support that we could get after her death. But we were hearing this while she was sat in the other room. The nurse was wonderful and I had always admired the Macmillan nurses but it was just too much.

I asked her how long Mum had left. She couldn't possibly give us an answer but it was never going to be months. Perhaps not even one. It was incomprehensible. I know that Sarah had picked up on the fact that my anger was getting the better of me. I felt guilty. I felt useless. And I was even starting to lose it when we were all sitting together in the lounge. Mum's breathing was not right. She was convulsing, her eyes would roll back into her head. This wasn't the Mum I knew. I was so angry at Cancer. I was angry at absolutely everything and everyone. I would clench my fists and I had to walk out of the room several times, which Mum was beginning to pick up on. *She can't see me like this.*

After a discussion with Sarah I agreed with the family that I would go back to London for one night. It felt like she was *my* older sister at this point. I felt ashamed. *I should be looking after her.* I needed to explain to work that I had to take time off and that I had no idea how long for. I would go back to my flat and pack up my things. I would take a night to calm myself down and return to Dorset and be the daughter that my mum deserved. Not this absolute mess that was stomping around about to burst. And I know it might sound crazy. I know that everyone will say, how could I leave? But you have to trust me on this one. I was doing it for her.

So I went. I went and I composed myself. I crashed for the night after seeing some friends and my housemates. *I still can't believe what I am saying out loud to them. I* didn't talk about it in too much detail. *I don't have the energy and I have no idea what I can say anyway.*

The next morning I spoke to HR and then I headed back to the coach station at Victoria. As I was boarding the coach, I bumped into an old school friend. I couldn't have been happier to see a familiar face. She asked me how I was. The poor girl asked me how I was. She was so shocked and saddened to hear what was happening. A while into the journey, the driver announced that we had hit some traffic and were going to be considerably late. Dad called me and, as I answered, I could sense the panic in his voice. He asked me to hurry up. *Let me off this coach.* Mum had been asking where I was. But I was stuck. I was in traffic and I wished I had never left home. I asked Dad to stop worrying and that I would be there soon. I asked if she was in a bad way and he told me that he thought it wouldn't be long. The traffic wasn't moving and neither was my heart. *What if something happens and I am not there?* This was the most agonising journey that I had ever experienced. I wanted to get off the coach and run. The adrenaline would get me there quicker. My friend tried to reassure me that I would get there eventually. *I hope so.*

The minute I got to the front door, an hour later than I should have been there, I dropped my bag and ran straight to find Mum and I hugged her — carefully, of course, as I knew that she was in a huge amount of pain. I sat with her and held her hand. I kept it together. I didn't show her that I was broken.

I asked Hannah what had happened since I had been gone and she told me about a very funny moment they'd had. *Of course, it was Hannah talking after all!* The medical bed arrived and Hannah sat down on it while Mum pressed the button to rise her up as high as she could. Hannah still laughs her head off when she tells this story. It makes me happy that no matter how many drugs she was taking, how much she did not seem like my mum anymore, she was still there really.

In all this time, since she had first fallen ill, my mother had not complained once. Not once. She told me that at least she had been able to marry Dad and had been able to have us three girls. That she had enjoyed such a wonderful life with us. It seemed so final to hear her speak like that. But she was so positive. And she went on to say that so many children have cancer and how sad that was. She was still thinking of other people.

We had no chance of any 'lasts' with Mum. No chance of whisking her off to a tropical island or taking her to see a show or even the cinema. There was no way she could make it outside. She couldn't eat and she couldn't drink so we couldn't even enjoy a last meal together. We just had to sit with her. Sit and hold her hand and watch her die. And the worst thing for me was that she knew she was going. This had all happened so suddenly and, because of that, very few people were able to come round to say goodbye. My poor mum knew that she was leaving everyone that she loved behind her. And everyone she loved was losing her.

The words 'chemotherapy', 'radiotherapy' and 'benign' were the words that I had previously associated with cancer. But these words were never going to make it into our vocabulary. We all knew that my mother was a fighter. But in order to prove yourself to be a great fighter, you need to be given a challenge — a chance. It was as if Mum was in a boxing ring, with her family, her friends — everyone — around her, psyching her up for the battle

51

ahead. But her opponent, 'The Big C', couldn't even be bothered to come out of the dressing room. The coward refused to get into the ring. The fight was over before it could begin.

Saturday 11th February, 2012 — The third phone call

I woke up thinking that it was just the day after the one before. I went down to make a coffee. I said morning to Mum, who seemed to be much worse. It was at this point that I started to get more and more scared to be around her. And, believe me, it kills me to say that. She was so far from the mum that I knew so well, the mum I had known all twenty-eight years of my life. She was getting more and more dazed and confused under the drugs that she was on and I just wished so much that I could have a normal conversation with her. The speed of the deterioration was unreal — I had never heard of anything like it. But we had to watch it. She was fading with every single struggle of a breath. The atmosphere in the house on that morning was one of panic. But it always seemed a calm panic. No one raised their voice, there were no signs of anger. We had been warned we were looking at a sooner-rather-than-later prognosis and, with this in mind, I wanted to put in place a trail of messengers. Three of my closest friends would deliver the news and filter it out to others when the time came. What a bleak job. I knew I would be in no fit state to do it. No way on earth.

Facebook
10.57am

Hi ladies,
I hope you are well and enjoying the week-end. It's sunny today which is bloody lovely!
Getting straight to the point, it is very traumatic times down here. Mum can no longer walk, hold a conversation . . . she is drugged up to the max, convulsing all the time. It won't be long until she doesn't know who we are. We've had two nurses and a doctor around already today as Mum can no longer swallow so they are deciding what to do re: drug intake.
So, as I already discussed briefly with Becs and Caroline, I wondered if you girls could help me in preparation for the inevi-table. When it happens I would be ever so grateful if you three could help me with fil-tering the news.

Caroline, if you could let the work lot know . . . perhaps the core people at first and then I guess they will filter it out to the others at work. I will contact Marcus and Cat myself though.

Becs if you could take the Treaties and Vivan crew [house mates old and new] and anyone else that you feel should know.

Bethan, please may you tell the Shirelings [Dorset school friends] and your girlies . . . I will tell Beth myself.

Sorry for the utterly depressing Facebook message. Please all have fabulous Saturday nights! Jaegers! Sarah and I are just off to Wimborne Market to hunt for empty jars as she has decided she has an urge to make caramelised red onion chutney. Well, of course! Haha!

Loving you girls with all of my heart. This is going to be ok.

Rach xxxxxxxxxxxxxxxxx

Reading that back not only brought me to tears but also enraged me. Does it sound like someone who is waiting for their mother to die? No. Does it sound like someone who is absolutely beside themselves with panic, helplessness and fear? No — it really doesn't. I sound so goddarn cheery. Well, I can tell you, that is the opposite of how I was *actually* feeling. *I am more scared than I have ever been in my life.* Even though it was my closest friends, who I always feel that I can be so honest with, I was still putting on a front. Instinct was already kicking in. I suppose when I was saying, 'This is going to be OK,' I wasn't talking to them. I was talking to myself. *It has to be OK — somehow.*

I hit send to the message not knowing just how soon it would be that I would need their help.

As Sarah and I were on our way out of the front door to get her chutney jars, we shouted to Dad, 'Do you need us to pick anything up?' 'An *Echo* please,' Dad replied. The *Daily Echo* was our local paper and, in keeping with a family joke that Dad had started years ago, we heard — incredibly — a shout from Mum, 'ECHO!' That warmed my heart. She could hear us, she could understand us, and she was telling a joke — Mum was still Mum.

We arrived at Wimborne Market and, as we walked up through the first stretch of stalls, my phone rang. I knew. Sarah knew. It was the third and final phone call. I pressed to answer. It was Dad. He delivered the inevitable words that I never wanted to hear, 'She's gone.'

Sixteen days — just two weeks and two days — is the short amount of time you can take off work to go on your annual summer break. It can be the amount of time it takes to get a doctor's appointment or the time it takes for a parcel to get from one side of the world to the other. For me, sixteen days will always be the heart-wrenchingly short period of time between my mother being diagnosed with cancer and the day that we lost her. *It sends a shiver down my spine.* Sixteen days. Just SIXTEEN DAYS. I still can't get my head around it and I point-blank refuse to.

It took just two weeks and two days for my mum's life to be snatched away from her. And for my dad, my two sisters and me life would never be the same again.

4

Life As We (Don't) Know It

It was thirteen long days from the date that Mum died until her funeral — only three days less than the time between her diagnosis and death. But it was in this very time, strangely, that I finally began to pull myself together and support the family. Something I should have done for those weeks before.

Flashbacks of the day she died were rife in my mind. The look on Sarah's face as I took that final call from my dad. Having to walk with her back along the stalls and to the car with people watching as we walked. Driving down our cul-de-sac to find Dad waiting for us outside. Him embracing us both on the driveway as we walked up to the house. That was the first moment since the phone call that I began to cry — in my dad's arms. Until then I had felt numb. I can remember vividly the panic we felt that Hannah wasn't there yet. *Where is she?* She was driving over to see Mum when it had happened; she didn't know. But she knew as soon as she came to the door. My heart was breaking for everyone. *This can't be real.*

We never speak of what happened in the house when Mum died. All I know is that my mum did not die in her sleep, as I know that my dad and Aunty Anne had to rush into the room that she was in. If that despicable disease was aggressive enough and moving so quickly to prevent any single hope of treatment — for there to be nothing in the world that they could do — then it was most likely a horrific ending to a very traumatic time for my poor mum. I know my dad was relieved that my sisters and I had not been there. I have heard so many stories since about people who wait for their loved ones to be safely at a distance before letting themselves pass away, in order to protect them from the pain of having to watch it happen. There was barely a moment when one of us was not in the house, yet the moment she went, none of her girls were by her side. We think that she did this to protect us. And Dad, as part of our parenting team, has done the same by not bringing that difficult time up. *This will be the last I speak of it — my heart will never be able to cope with it. I know that.*

Our family friend and doctor, Andy, had been called over to report the time of death.

Mum looked so peaceful, which was a comfort after the pain I had seen her in, but I couldn't stay in that room for long. She looked like she was sleeping, except her body was getting colder by the minute and I couldn't help but feel that I could sit there forever waiting for her to wake up. *Mum? MUM!* It was the worst goodbye I have ever had to say. I can't imagine I will ever have a worse one. But what was even more heart-rending was hearing everyone else saying their final words to her. Especially Dad's — that was unbearable. I called Hannah's fiancé, Joe, to tell him what had happened — that our nightmare had become a reality. He said that he would come over straight away. He was the first person that I delivered the news to and I shivered at the thought of just how many times I would have to repeat the devastating news. *Over and over again.*

No ambulance was needed — there were no paramedics in sight. *It's too late.* We just had the undertakers to call. They arrived an hour after she died and advised us to close the lounge door and the curtains for the next stage. I wished that we had put on some music because I could hear the haunting sound of the body bag being zipped up and the wheels of the stretcher carrying her out to the car to be taken to the morgue. There is nothing in this world that can prepare you for that experience. *I can't believe she is gone.*

In the afternoon, after making a few phone calls (*I never noticed how sad a voice could sound*) I went back to my mum's favourite view down on Evening Hill. I sat, I cried, I clenched my fists with anger — I was despairing, in pure disbelief — my body shaking in a state of utter shock. But I told myself that I could no longer let myself slip as I had done in the previous weeks. I needed to make a change. It was from this point forward that something inside me sparked both my mind and body into action. I had been so angry and helpless during my mother's last two weeks and it was time to step up and support my family. *They need me.*

Waking up on the first morning without Mum was horrendous. I heard a noise downstairs in the kitchen and my immediate thought was that it was her — but it couldn't be. *My heart sank.* I went down to find my dad tidying and cleaning and telling us we must crack on. *I miss her so much already. It hurts.* We went down to the beach for breakfast. It all felt so unreal but I was glad to be by the sea once more — my escape.

In the afternoon I called Caroline. I know that she was expecting me to be in pieces but instead I was calling her from inside a sports shop and asking her advice on which trainers I should buy. I had decided that I needed to run more. *Obviously.* I could hear the surprise in her voice. I know that I was in complete denial and doing everything that I could to forget the pain of the day before and the pain that was going to be part of my life from now on. *Keep going. You have to keep going.* I chose some trainers at random and headed for the counter. 'I will take these ones please,' I beamed at the shop assistant, who could have no idea that twenty-four hours ago my mother had died. *See — I can do this.*

As soon as the first day without Mum was over it was Project Management Time for me as I reminded myself of my pep talk on Evening Hill. There were things to be done — there were *so* many things to be done. You associate death with emotion. I was trying to put that aside because I wasn't ready to face up to how I was feeling (or not feeling). I had to deal with the other side of death to keep my mind off things. It was a side to death that I had no idea would be such hard work — the admin. *They really don't make this any easier for you.*

My dad had so much paperwork to fill in — I tried to help as best I could. I was shocked to find how costly it all was, too. I mean, you have just gone through the most horrendous thing in your life and then you have thousands of pounds taken out of your account. *Not OK.* We had to close all of her accounts and it was when I asked the family about Mum's Marks and Spencer's card that I found out it had already been sorted. *How is this possible?* Mum had done it herself before she passed away. *Oh, Mum.* Yet another brutal reminder that she knew exactly what was happening. She knew the inevitable and it was typical of her to try to help us in advance. She was selfless until the very end.

The next task of my self-appointed admin role was something that I decided I had to do on my own. I was going to go to Mum's school and clear her classroom. I felt that with my newfound strength (even if it was just a mask) and, bearing in mind the fact that I was now less associated with the area (living in London), I thought it was something that I should deal with. Not to mention the fact that both Dad and Sarah were teachers. It would be too much for them.

It was half-term the week after Mum died — I would not have to face anyone at school. *That is a relief.* And, knowing my mum as well as I do, she had probably been trying to help the children by dying when they weren't there. After all, she had done that for us. I called up my mum's good friend and work colleague Liz just six days after Mum had passed, to ask if she could get me access into the school and to help me with Mum's classroom. Now this is where my organisational role was causing me to be blind-sighted. When I called Liz, she had listened to my request and, without a moment's hesitation, said she would be there. I was so sure that this was what I needed to do that it hadn't even crossed my mind how horrendously tough this was going to be for her. I should have realised it would be extremely painful for her to visit the place that she was so used to seeing Mum. *What was I thinking? My family were not the only ones who were grieving. I must not forget that.*

As I opened Mum's classroom door I got the fright of my life. *What the — ?* There was a candle lit on her desk — I didn't think anyone had been in but the caretaker had placed it there. It was such a beautiful touch. I knew that this would be just the first of many candles lit in her memory. As I looked around the classroom, I noticed so many things that I recognised — photos up on the walls, her pens and her notepads. *How she loved her pretty notepads.* But I think it was seeing her handwriting that shook me the most. We packed up a box and even managed to have a giggle at the secret stash of chocolate goodies that she had hidden in her store cupboard. She had jackets in there, too — they smelt like Mum. It was far too soon for me to find any of this a comfort, though — not when things were so raw. We realised that her laptop would have to be handed back to the school. It would be full of marking and reports. And, of course, lesson plans — lessons that she would never teach.

I took Mum's box home and unpacked it on the kitchen table. I found her laptop and put it to one side and tried desperately to remember her password. *Why don't I know it?* My mask of strength was still on, but I was no superhero. Behind that mask lay a broken human being. I looked forward to an early night and a weekend of battling on. *I have to keep this up — the mask cannot slip.* The weekend ahead didn't feel like a 'weekend' anymore. I hadn't known what day it was for the past month. All I knew was that every day that passed was another day without seeing my mum. And, to make matters worse, on Monday afternoon I was to face the next gruelling task on my to-do list. *This is relentless.*

The Vicar sent me the order of service by email for the family to approve. The subject read 'Viv Chadwick'. That was a bad start. Ridiculous as it may sound, despite knowing that I was receiving the email on the Monday before Mum's funeral, for a millisecond I did wonder . . . *No — obviously it can't be her.* And there I was — looking at a list of what would happen during the funeral. I had organised so many events before with an itinerary — this one looked so odd. 'Hymns, reading, tribute, music out.' This was the worst event that I could ever attend, let alone have a hand in organising. And so I responded, 'The Order of Service looks great, thank you.' *Great? Who am I kidding? It looks horrendous.*

In the week leading up to that dreaded service, there was not a day that went by when the mat at the front door was not piled high with cards and letters. We sat down and began to go through the messages of condolence — we counted up to three hundred. *Wow.* But it should not have been a surprise, really — Mum was loved by so many. And rarely did they enclose just an 'I'm sorry' (not that it would be a bad thing if they had). Most were full of words and memories of Mum. Just as I had found with my visit to her classroom, I was not ready to 'look back' with happy thoughts. *I wonder when or even whether that time will come.*

The house had turned into a florist — everywhere you looked was another bouquet. We had far more flowers than we had vases, that was for sure. I found the smell overwhelming as well as the thought that, just like Mum, they blossomed with life until their inevitable end. *I'm not sure I will ever look at flowers in the same way.* In preparation for the impending funeral, rather than people sending flowers, we asked for donations to the Victoria Spark Appeal, which is a specialist school, offering education, therapy and nursing to children with physical disabilities, in our local area. It was a charity that was very close to Mum's heart as she had a link with them through her school and had made several trips on activities' weeks taking children over there to help.

I decided that I would do something special for the wake. We had so many amazing photos of Mum from past and present — from when she was a child, when we were children, of family holidays and photos of her with friends. I collected them all up and made photo boards of memories, borrowing large display boards from Mum's school just a couple of days before the funeral. I stuck on the photos in chronological order and couldn't help but snigger at the sight of the retro-look eighties shots. I found it hard to be looking at Mum everywhere, though. Especially as she looked so fit and well in all the photos. My memories of her were still of how she had looked when she was in her final days. *I hope they go away.* Once the photos were done, the funeral organisation was complete — we were all set for Friday. *As ready as we could be.*

The day of the funeral arrived and it was exactly one month and one day from when Mum had first been diagnosed. *I am lost in the timelessness.* As we all got ready for the funeral that morning, it felt strange and almost wrong to be getting dressed up for such an event. But we decided that we had to look our best for Mum — to look smart for her send-off. *Send-off sounds so final. Because it is.* My dad had arranged for the coffin to be in the church already. The service was taking place at Wimborne Minster in the centre of the local town. The church had been part of our childhood — from visits with Dad's parents, our Granny and Grandpa, to school concerts we had all been a part of. It is such a beautiful building right next to the green and just moments away from where Mum had taught — it was the only option for us. *This is where she would want it to be.*

While travelling in the car, we remained very quiet, watching all the other cars on the road stop in sympathy to let us through. My head was telling me to be strong but my body was telling me that nothing was going to stop me shaking. I was adamant that I would at least make it to my seat without breaking down — I had to hold it together. *Please hold it together.* When we arrived we could see that there were still people flooding through the entrance to the church and we waited until everyone was in. The clock struck eleven and it was time for us to be escorted to our seats.

As I walked down the aisle I felt sick as all eyes were on us — staring in sorrow. I tried to avoid eye contact with anyone and looked ahead, only to find myself faced with the harrowing, harsh sight of my mother's coffin. I tried to thank my dad, telepathically, for not making us endure any more time looking at that than we had to. The less time spent around the wooden casket holding my mother's dead body, the better. *I hate it.* As we took our places in the pew, we picked up the Order of Service — a photo of Mum skiing smiled at us on the front. This was going to be insufferable. *You have to keep it together.* I didn't know where to look. I didn't want to see the smiling photo of Mum, nor the coffin, or anyone in the building, for that matter. I held Sarah's hand tightly. I was at the end of the pew and suddenly wished that there had been a person to my right with an arm around me, holding me — not a cold, hard pillar.

The service began and it was so far so good (as good as it could be), until the first hymn. I couldn't see the page in front of me anymore, my Order of Service became wet with tears and my voice could no longer sing a note. I looked to my left and glanced at a group of my friends from both my childhood and my London life. The floodgates opened even more. I don't know why I was beating myself up about it so much. *It is my mother's funeral* — cry.

A close family friend called Paul — someone who knew my mum and dad very well — stood up at the lectern and gave the most stunning eulogy for Mum. He delivered it with such strength, poise, humility, and was even able to add a pinch of wit, which she would have appreciated so much. We were all so touched by his words. Then it was Uncle Michael, my dad's sister's husband, who stood up and walked to the front. He recited words that I have grown to love so much:

She Is Gone

You can shed tears that she is gone
Or you can smile because she has lived
You can close your eyes and pray that
    she will come back
Or you can open your eyes and see all
    that she has left
Your heart can be empty because you
    can't see her
Or you can be full of the love that you
    shared
You can turn your back on tomorrow
    and live yesterday
Or you can be happy for tomorrow
    because of yesterday
You can remember her and only that she
    is gone
Or you can cherish her memory and let it
    live on
You can cry and close your mind, be
    empty and turn your back
Or you can do what she would want:
    smile, open your eyes, love and go on.
David Harkins

This was a beautiful choice of poem. So positive, so focussed on the memories, about looking forward and doing what she would want — this was perfect for Mum.

Dad had chosen the song that would be

played as the coffin was carried out. It was an Irish song by Lunasa, one that my mum had adored. It was an upbeat song and Dad had hoped that this would leave people smiling on the way out. Smiling for Mum.

I wanted to smile on the way out, too, but, as we followed the coffin back down the aisle, I looked up and I noticed the sea of school uniforms before me. They were Allenbourn Middle School students, all wearing their uniforms in Mum's honour. The school had closed for the day so that children, teachers and parents could visit Wimborne Minster and say their goodbyes. We were truly touched. Sobbing as I walked out of the church, I thought about how she would have been so happy that they were all able to attend.

The next call was the crematorium for the second ceremony. We followed the coffin in the car and we were once again thrown into deadly silence. *Please give me a break.* With only immediate family around us and not hundreds as in the church — this was far more difficult. Everywhere I turned there was someone that was so close to Mum — everyone's eyes were wet with tears. *I need this ceremony to be over now.* We had decided not to get the coffin lowered at the end of the service. They give you the option

71

— *thank goodness*. We were in complete agreement that the coffin was to stay exactly where it was. *I already hate the idea of her body being burned. I do not want the reminder.*

We visited Wimborne Cemetery where Mum's ashes were to be buried, then headed for Allendale Community Centre where everyone had gathered for the wake. I was so delighted to see everyone standing around the photo boards, and with smiles on their faces, too. It had slipped my mind just how many people attending that day would find their face up on that memory montage. *I'm glad I did it.*

I was overwhelmed by how many of my friends had come to pay their respects and to support me on that day. Some of these friends had never even met my mum and had only heard about her from me. That blew me away — that they would come all this way to say goodbye. I was so busy during the wake (which I suppose is a good thing for distraction purposes) that I barely got a chance to speak to any of my friends properly. But it was such a comfort that every time I looked around the room, I could see they were there.

One person who I was dying to see (perhaps not the best choice of words) was my Aunty Tinky. Well, she isn't actually my aunty — she is my godmother. And she isn't actually called Tinky — she is called Anita. But Aunty Tinky was how I always knew her. She was Mum's best friend and when I saw her I just wanted to cry immediately. Tink had moved away many years ago with her husband and three beautiful little children to the Isle of Islay in Scotland. Although many years had passed, she was always a part of our family. Unfortunately it was just before Mum was diagnosed that Tinky got in touch to say that she was moving back. Mum and Tink had been emailing and, eventually, as Mum became too weak to do it, I had taken over as she told me what to type. Mum was deteriorating so rapidly they never had a chance to be reunited. But their bond was strong. Mum knew that Tink would understand. And she also knew that I would keep in touch and keep our families together. That was an unspoken promise. Aunty Tinky and I hugged for a long while and both tried not to let our emotions take over too much. I knew this wasn't going to be the time or the place for a long catch-up, but she was back in my life now and there would be plenty of other opportunities.

I think the most uncomfortable that I felt at the wake, was when I met people who I had never seen before. It was difficult to comprehend that so many people had been in Mum's life and, of course, I understood that I could not possibly know them all. But I also felt a twinge of jealousy when I realised that some people had spent so much more time with her than I had, since I moved away to London. *I want her back. I want more time with her.*

As everyone started to leave, we could all breathe a sigh of relief. We had made it through the day and we had given Mum the best possible send-off that we could. Dad had invited the family and our closest friends back to our house for drinks and nibbles afterwards. I felt completely exhausted. I felt as though my sisters and I had put on the biggest show ever performed. If anyone had walked into that wake, I don't think that they would have believed that we were the daughters of the deceased. *We are, though — and I, for one, was feeling this mask getting heavier and causing me more pain each day.*

It was only a few days later that Dad called a family meeting in the lounge. As he had a job as a headteacher, he decided that he wanted to get back to work — to get stuck in and to keep himself busy. He declared, in his headteacher voice, that we should no longer be sat at home wallowing and instead we should do what Mum would have wanted and get back to it. He wanted to get back into a daily routine, throwing himself into his job. And so, I packed my bags, said my incredibly emotional goodbyes and I was on my way back to London once more. Except this time, I didn't have a mother.

⋆ ⋆ ⋆

Sitting at my desk in the office after just five weeks off, it felt all wrong. In the short time in which I had been absent from work, we had found out that Mum had cancer, been told there was nothing that they could do, spent a gruelling two weeks and two days watching her die and had organised and attended her funeral. Going back to reality was, quite simply, incomprehensible. There was no going back after what we had been through. *How was I going to do it?* Nothing felt real at all as I recognised the fact that I was still in a state of complete and utter shock. And I didn't know if I would ever pull myself out of it.

I had pre-warned my closest friends about how nervous I was about coming back to London life. I was very reluctant to go on as normal. I didn't want to pretend that everything was OK but deep down I knew that I had to — that it was the only way I would be able to get through. And you know what? I think I put on a very good performance.

I had assumed and desperately hoped that word about my news had spread around the office while I was gone, because I just couldn't face telling people and saying those words out loud just yet. *I need more practice.* I knew it would break me, cause *me* to break down in front of others. I needed to keep the facade up, that I was doing well. I practised in my head over and over how I would tell them if I had to, but it was hard enough just doing that. Low and behold, the news had skipped some people and it was on speaking to them that I was faced with the questions. 'Hey, Rach, have you been on holiday or something?' or 'Where have you been, I haven't seen you in a while?' *Dear black hole, please, please swallow me up right here, right now.*

It was clear that there was no way around this. I was going to have to face facts — some people simply did not know. It was people's reactions to me that I found (and continue to find) absolutely fascinating. It feels almost like a social experiment at times. I totally understand that there is a severe lack of guidance on What To Do When You Hear

Someone Has Died. You see, as the person who has lost someone, even you don't know what you want or need from other people. It can change on a daily basis. And if *you* don't know, how is anyone else supposed to know? There can be absolutely no right or wrong way to behave in times like this. How can there be when each of us is so different? I did not have one bad experience with anyone, nor did I judge anyone for any reaction I experienced. I have no idea how I would deal with it myself. But in those early days when I was more sensitive than ever, it seemed that every single reaction was difficult to take at first. And there were certain categories forming. *None of these were bad — remember that.*

The Avoiders

These people hope that you don't notice when they dodge out of your line of sight, but it's very hard not to. They try to stay in a different room to you and choose to say nothing. I imagine that it is the fear of not knowing what the best thing to say is, or even the fear of saying the wrong thing. Who can blame them? There is no rule book to follow.

The Criers

When someone cried to my face, I looked at it in two ways, depending on what my own behaviour had been. If I was crying, then it was fair enough if they cried, too — I felt comforted by their empathy. If I wasn't crying, then it put me in the difficult position of feeling I should be comforting *them*. I already had enough people to look after. *Please, please wipe your tears.*

The Huggers

A hug should be reciprocal. It should be a mutual embrace that at least comes with some kind of warning. But sometimes I would find myself standing there as someone clung to me, which is not the most comfortable of situations. *I feel a little trapped here!*

The Tilters

Oh now I am getting a little picky — but my, oh my, the head tilts that I had to endure! Team the tilt with a bottom lip out and sympathy eyes — it is just so sad to look at that head tilt. It almost made me feel sad, too.

The Cliché Users

'Time is a healer' and 'It will get better in time' they told me. This was so difficult to hear because I felt guilty at the thought that I would one day feel better without Mum around. But I hoped that they were right. *This cannot get any worse.*

The Suffer Police

According to this type of person, the fact that it was just two weeks and two days from my mum's diagnosis to death is, apparently, a good thing. It means that she didn't suffer for long. Unfortunately this does not make me feel any better. If the cancer was spreading that quickly, I cannot even begin to imagine how much she suffered.

The Disbelievers

I completely understand that when people say they are surprised I am carrying on when they would be 'so devastated they would not be able to do anything', what they mean is, 'You are doing well.' And that is lovely. But sometimes it makes me feel as if what they are actually saying is, they would be more sad if it happened to them and, therefore, I am not sad enough.

I'm sorry

Now we come to the phrase that is most ingrained in our society as the 'done thing' to say when someone has died. 'I'm sorry.' I have always said that one, too, and I am sure I will again but, being on the other side of it and talking to others who have lost someone, too, I realise how difficult a sentence it is to respond to. You are tempted to say, 'It's OK.' But really it is anything but. I just find myself stuttering incoherently with a weak smile, ready to change the subject as quickly as I can.

And, finally, we come to what hurts the most. The silence — when people stop saying anything. Life for them carries on as usual while, behind closed doors, you are still working out how to put your heart back together with Sellotape. Because, undoubtedly, it will never be fully fixed again.

After three weeks, I met my best friend Caroline for lunch one day and she remembers the moment very clearly. I imagine she wished she had never shown up.

I ranted like an angry, red-faced monster that, 'NO ONE IS ASKING ME IF I AM OK!' I declared that I wanted to get a T-shirt printed stating, 'My mum died and I am not OK.' Perhaps, on reflection, there should be a second one in your bag for moments where you want to say, 'My mum died but I don't want you to mention it.'

I started to go to the local pub again near work and now I had to deal with just how much mothers come up in conversation. I had never even noticed before but it is almost a daily occurrence. *Mums are everywhere!* People talk about their mums, say that they need to call their mum, say they need their mum's advice, say they are going round to their mum's for Sunday dinner and they moan about their mums. *Mum, mum, mum!* The most awkward one of them all is when someone drops a 'Mum joke' on me. *Taxi for one.* The minute that it dawns on them that I am standing there, they stop mid-flow with panic on their faces and with mutterings of 'So sorry', they scuttle off to the bar. This makes everything so much more awkward. Because that is exactly it — it is more awkward for other people than it is for the person who has lost someone. I do not want anyone to stop talking about their mothers on my account. I would never want other people to stop talking about their mums because I want to be able to talk about mine, too.

It was not long after my lunch with Caroline that I had to face up to the technological side of grief. Mum's name was still in my phone. I deliberated time after time whether or not it would be better to delete it but I came to the conclusion that it would be too final. And, to be honest, I felt so sad at not being able to talk to her that I had started sending her messages. *I still do.*

But every time I typed 'V' (for Vivienne) in the 'To' field of my email account, her address would appear right in front of me. It was incessant. Every single Next of Kin form that I had ever filled in had her details sprawled all over it. And the final blow came when I realised that almost every security password I had contained her maiden name — 'Love'. 'Ah, what a lovely name,' people would say as I answered.

Something had to be done. In a very calm and collected way I insisted to the poor lady on the other end of the phone at the bank that she had to make sure that the security question — What is your mother's maiden name — was removed with immediate effect. She said it wasn't possible. I explained. She made it possible. I thanked her. And I thanked her even more in my head when I remembered just how many bank cards I go through.

After I had dealt with all of the above, I felt a shiver as I passed the shop windows, realising what was on its way — Mother's Day. *Right — I've had enough.* I needed to get out of the country, pronto. So that is exactly what I did. I asked the family if it was OK and, with great understanding, they told me that I had to do what was best for me.

I told Caroline that I felt a sudden urge to run away and, in true friendship style, she was in it with me. Within four days we were booked, packed and heading to Gatwick Airport for a four-day trip to Barcelona. This was exactly what I needed. The fact that we had booked an apartment that required you to open the door while you were still inside the lift was a very good start — it was a totally novel experience and provided a lot of entertainment. *This is amazing!* We soaked up the culture (and soaked up the wine with a lot of bread), we spent hours on end just sitting in silence reading our books, we ate good food and I barely talked about Mum at all. I was emotionally exhausted and just wanted a break from the real world. Well, what was left of my real world. *Very little, or so it felt.*

It was on the way back home on the flight

that it all came back to bite me. A scramble for seats had left Caroline and me separated. I wandered up and down the aisle trying to find any sign of a space. At one point I thought I might have to sit in the toilet. *That would be just my luck!* Finally I was able to grab one at the very front. After being angered at the fact that the air steward had made a song and dance about me putting my scarf in the overhead compartment (*oh — come on!*), it started to dawn on me that I was going home. But I wasn't going home to life as I once knew it. I may have buried my head in the sand about everything for the past four days, but now I was going back and my mum still wasn't there.

Unfortunately, despite having an amazing escape for a few days, I was very much back to how I was before I left within a few hours of landing on home soil. I know that there is a theory about the five stages of grief: denial, anger, bargaining, depression and acceptance. I haven't done much reading up on it but, in my experience, these come in no particular order, sometimes in threes or on occasions all at once. On that flight home I experienced such strong emotions which I had totally no control over. It was the first time it had happened and I had absolutely no idea when the next phase would come. (*I still don't.*)

On top of the lack of control over how, when or what I was feeling, I discovered something else over which I was powerless — my sleep. I knew that having a good rest would help — but I just couldn't. I was lucky to get more than three hours a night. I tried sleeping pills and lavender oil (which did end up working the best for me) but there was no stopping my dreams. I have always suffered from bad nightmares and sometimes even night terrors, but now I had to watch my mother die again every time I closed my eyes for sleep. And you know when you wake up sobbing but you calm yourself down with the realisation that everything is OK? I can't begin to explain the fear when, instead of that calming process on waking, you realise that it isn't OK. She really is gone. It is like receiving the news all over again. *I don't want to fall asleep.*

I had to adjust my body to the sleep deprivation and accept that it wasn't going away any time soon. That worry was put to one side as next on the agenda was the first family birthday — it was Dad's. I went back home to be with the family and there was a sense of sadness as we gave him his card and present. There was no 'Happy' about it with his leading lady missing. I worried about how it would be for my sisters when their birthdays came around. I worried about mine, too. Maybe it would be better by then, as they were months away? Then again, maybe not.

Just after Dad's birthday I had my first work party to go to since everything had happened. I usually thrive at these parties, especially as I was on the organising committee. But I felt anxious and scared and it came as a surprise — I loved being social and didn't want large groups to start to be a problem. I felt like I was becoming less and less my normal self and I was growing increasingly tired of putting up a front. I guess it was partly because, at this point, I was aware that some people *still* didn't know. It made me worry about meeting new people, as well, something which I used to love to do so much. I wasn't dating at the time and I was happy about that — I didn't want to put all of this on someone else — but I worried that I was going to be afraid of letting anyone in. *Ever.*

Thankfully there was a bright shining star in the distance that was keeping me afloat. There was something to look forward to. A family event was on its way and I had to stay strong and work with them to make it a day to remember.

5

My Little Sister's Wedding

It was all systems go on the morning of Saturday 9th June, 2012. It was the day of my little sister Hannah's wedding. Hairpins and make-up brushes were flying everywhere, not to mention the hold-in pants and the strapless bras. Poor Dad tried to stay well out of it — wisely so. Coffee and tea mugs were piling up and then out came the bubbly to keep us all going and to calm the nerves. When I say that, I mean my nerves. *I'm a wreck!* Hannah was doing a grand job of keeping her cool. Meanwhile, I was in a rush to get ready. (Why change the habit of a lifetime?) *I blame the frizzy hair — L'Oréal would definitely not think my barnet was worth it.*

Sarah and I were playing the role of bridesmaids along with the groom's sisters, Megan and Hettie, and Hannah's best friend, Dani, who was assigned Chief Bridesmaid responsibilities. *No, of course, I wasn't jealous in the slightest. Why would you think that?*

The atmosphere in the house that morning, despite being a little hectic, was generally very upbeat and excitable. This was very good news. We were all so desperate to make this the best day for Hannah. The best day that it could possibly be with such a hugely heart-breaking and noticeable absence of one very important lady.

Hannah confessed to me that she had got up at the crack of dawn and snuck down to the lounge to have a moment. She calls it the, 'Where are you, Mum?' moment, as she struggled to face the fact that Mum would not be there to help her get ready, do up her dress and see her marry the love of her life. My protective older sister and maternal instinct (that I so often feel with Hannah being the youngest) kicked in and I wished that I had been there to sit with her. But she assured me that it was something that she had to do by herself. She needed to clear her head and prepare herself for the day.

One of Hannah's strongest memories of a time spent alone with Mum before she passed was when they had watched *Mamma Mia* together. Mum had sobbed her heart out at the scene where the mother is brushing her daughter's hair on the morning of her wedding. At the time Hannah thought she was just being emotional. *Mum was a soppy one*. But, looking back, Hannah realised that, even though Mum hadn't been diagnosed when they watched the film, it was if Mum knew that she was not going to make it to the wedding. *How could she handle knowing that?*

Hannah had been so sure that Mum was going to be with us for longer than everyone was saying and so had thought about bringing the wedding forward. But little did she know it was a matter of days, not weeks. When Mum died, Hannah wondered if she should postpone the date — she wasn't sure that she could cope with the wedding while it was all still so raw. I didn't know what advice to give her, other than support her no matter what — it had to be whatever was best for Hannah and her heart. I knew that Mum wanted it to go ahead. In her last week she had looked at the table where the invitations were piled up and said to me in a calm and matter-of-fact tone, 'Make sure those go out, please.' It upset Hannah that Mum never mentioned the wedding during the sixteen days. But we all know that it would have broken them both to pieces. It would have been too much. *I wish I could help her.*

So my sister made the brave decision to keep the original date. I had asked to be responsible for the invitations — I wanted to play as much a part in the day as I could. I had sent the original image of the church and the whole design idea to my friend James, who I used to live with. As an architect, he had far better design programmes on his computer than I did. We still hadn't sent the invitations out when we lost Mum and there were so many deliberations as to whether the invites should stay as they were, but with so many friends and family coming, we could not work out what would be more painful for everyone — to see her name or to see her name missing. I sent a message to James to alter the design and they were changed to state just 'Mr P Chadwick invites . . . ' I visited the same printing shop in Marylebone as I had the first time around. Luckily they had not recognised me. This was not a situation that I wanted to explain. I couldn't have been more relieved that I was in charge of this task, though, and not Hannah. She had more than enough to deal with. They were beautiful invitations but now with a beautiful name removed. *My heart cannot stop breaking — for Hannah — for everyone.*

In the weeks leading up to the wedding, the church and the venue had been confirmed, the flowers sorted and the dresses had been fitted, so all that was left for the morning was to make sure that we looked the part. Hannah had her hair done and then her make-up, as the rest of us got in line to have our up-dos done. All the while, Dad was pottering around the house with a coffee in his hand. It made me laugh that, as we spent hours getting glammed up in our lounge-turned-salon, Dad, in the space of about ten minutes, had nipped upstairs, had a shower, a quick change and was good to go, looking very smart indeed. *Men have it so easy on the getting ready front.*

The fun mood around the place that morning was helped along with some comical moments. *Standard behaviour.* My own involved a tanning mishap. Deciding I was just a little too fair skinned (*what happened to being an English rose?*), I thought it would be a fantastic idea to slap on some tinted moisturiser. It would have been OK had I tested the brand beforehand. But, of course, I hadn't. I looked at myself in the bathroom mirror and could only wonder when I was going to get the call to be an extra in the next episode of *The Only Way Is Essex*. Luckily it wiped off pretty easily. *It might rain today. I can't risk it.*

Meanwhile Dani had experienced her own moment of madness. Dad had gone into the kitchen to find her at the back door shouting outside to Megan. Now, this doesn't sound too bad until I heard that she was lying on the floor bellowing through the cat-flap. I am still not quite sure why she chose not to open the door, but I'm glad she didn't — it provided hours of laughter both on the day and after!

The ribbon-draped vintage car arrived for the pick-ups and it was Megan and Hettie to go in the first run. Hettie, being slightly younger (*fine, a fair bit younger than me*), had been fretting about wearing such high heels all morning. 'Stop worrying, you will be fine!' we all reassured her. We had spoken too soon. As I was frantically attempting to detangle the necklace Hannah had given me and the other bridesmaids as a gift to wear, I heard fits of laughter from the driveway. I poked my head around the front door to find Hettie stuck in the metal drain. As she tried to yank her heel out, the drain came with her. *This is going to be an awkward walk down the aisle!* Luckily, with a little help from the driver of the car, she was freed and they were off. Just before Sarah and I took our journey to the church, the driver managed to fix my necklace, too. *Phew*. Now that is what you call going above and beyond.

As we pulled up outside Canford Magna Parish Church, set within a private school just next to the river, it looked magnificent. The sun was shining down brightly. I couldn't believe that after days and days of miserable wet weather, it had stopped for this special day. We did wonder if there was someone giving us a helping hand. *Thank you.*

As Dad helped the bride step out of the car, holding her dress carefully, I had a tear in my eye (*just don't tell her that*). She looked absolutely stunning. I know that every bride looks stunning — but Hannah was looking the most beautiful that I had ever seen her look. And, on top of that, when she had followed us down the aisle and taken her place opposite Joe, she was glowing with happiness.

I tried to keep my composure during the ceremony but the mention of those who were no longer with us and hearing the words 'till death us do part' left me a blubbering mess. *She should be here.* I couldn't help but look at Dad and wonder how he must be feeling — such an important family event and he did not have his wife by his side.

We all cheered as they pronounced Joe and Hannah 'Man and Wife' and, as they went off to sign the registry, it was my other sister, Sarah, who stepped up to the front of the church. Along with her friend who belonged to the same singing group, she sang Flower Duet — it was magical as their voices echoed beautifully around the church. It had been years since I had heard Sarah perform — only catching her singing along to the radio in the car or at home — and she blew me away. So many people flooded her with compliments as she sat back down. I was in awe of her. To get up and do that for Hannah and in front of so many people on such an emotional day was something I will always admire her for.

After (what felt like) a million photographs were taken outside the church, we were off in convoy to the reception venue. The Haven Hotel is in a stunning location, sat on the edge of the Sandbanks peninsula in Poole. It is right by the sea overlooking views of Old Harry Rocks in the distance and is just next to the little chain ferry that takes you over to Shell Bay, Studland and Swanage.

The drinks reception was held on the balcony and it was the first opportunity for the bride and groom, and the rest of us, to speak to the guests. It was lovely to see so many smiling faces around the room. I realised that the last time we had seen most of these people was at Mum's funeral and I was glad that we had something positive to celebrate together after a very sad year so far.

We sat down for a delicious three-course dinner and the wine was now flowing nicely. There was a tension in the air on the Head Table as the men prepared for speech time. I teased Dad and told him that maybe he should slow his wine flow but he laughed, politely told me to shut up and said it would be OK. I think this was the moment that I was the most nervous about — it was time for the Father of the Bride to speak. My dad stood tall, notes held tight in his hand, he took a deep breath and then he went against all of the odds and delivered the speech without a stutter. He said the most beautiful words about Mum to begin with and then moved on to some upbeat and witty stories about Hannah: her love for tomato ketchup (*there is nothing that she wouldn't try to drown in it*) and, my personal favourite, the time that she went through a McDonald's drive-through in an imaginary car. *I'm laughing too much — I've got a stitch.* He ended the speech by saying how much we love Joe and how he is such a perfect partner to Hannah.

Joe (*don't call him Joseph — he hates that — Broseph is even worse*) has been part of our family for years. He is such a great match for my baby sister — they are best friends and are there for each other no matter what. And, during the traumatic times that we went through, he not only supported Hannah but also the whole family. And for that we will be eternally grateful. *I now have a brother — brilliant.*

Hannah was such an elegant bride. Oh wait — let me rephrase that — Hannah was such an elegant bride until around eight o'clock when I found her on the dance floor with her shoes kicked off and the air guitar well and truly out. *If they need inspiration for Bridesmaids 2 the film — they need look no further.* She was throwing some shapes I had never seen before. *That's my girl.* It may have looked like *Strictly Come Dancing* on acid — but this meant that she was most definitely having a great night. *Shoes off — if you can't beat them* . . . We all danced together like no one was watching and I wished the night could go on forever.

This was a wedding that my mum would have been so proud of. I know Hannah still hurts, and always will, because Mum wasn't there. But Mum got to know Joe so well over the years and she had seen Hannah in her wedding dress, helped choose the brides-maids outfits and had even seen the church and the hotel. Mum really was a huge part of that special day. *And always will be.*

★ ★ ★

Hannah's wedding gave me a new lease of life. I was so proud of her and of the whole family, extended included, for coming together as a force to stay strong for Mum. Things were definitely beginning to feel a little brighter. I could only hope that it would continue.

We waved goodbye to Hannah and Joe as they went off on their honeymoon to Lake Como and it left Sarah and I preparing for a race we had entered the following weekend. It was a five-kilometre Race for Life event for Cancer Research UK that we were running in memory of Mum. Now, when I say that we were preparing for it, I mean Sarah was doing a better job than me. I had thought about running a lot as I walked all over London but I seemed to have a problem with breaking that walk into a jog. I had probably only done about two big runs before the main event. *Oh dear.* I told myself that I would be fitter next time. *I bet I repeat that phrase a few times!*

We called ourselves 'Team Love' after Mum and were delighted that nine of our friends signed up to join the group and run it with us. The Race is known for all things pink and so we stocked up on luminous T-shirts, leg warmers, sunglasses and the like. We met in Bournemouth and had to do a quick change into our running gear in a department store's toilets. *Classy, I know.* We decided to brand ourselves on our faces so scrawled 'Love' across our cheeks. It was only when we turned to look at each other that we noticed we had written it on in reflection — it was the wrong way around. *School girl error — start again*.

Bournemouth pier was a sea of pink — thousands of others were there already, all set and ready to run for the cause. Spirits were high and I was trying to look around for Sarah in the crowd when someone stepped in my way. It was the local radio. They stuck a microphone in my face. *Talk about putting a girl on the spot*. Before I knew it my voice was booming out of the speakers as I told them our team name and that we had managed to raise just over five thousand pounds. I thought it would be a good opportunity to find Sarah so did a shoutout for her. I can't believe I did that — it still makes me cringe. And, to add insult to injury, Sarah wasn't even listening. *Note to self: don't embarrass yourself on radio again*.

The fun-time warm-up was starting and I was already feeling a bit tired. *Uh oh!* We had our picture taken for the *Daily Echo* and then we were off to the starting line right on the beach front. We had made a pact as a group to run the whole thing together, no matter what, so we kept to a steady (snail's) pace. Some of us took it in turns to run ahead a bit, we were chanting and whooping and high-fiving the speed demons who were already on their way back before we had made it halfway. I think it's safe to say that we could have quite happily stayed at the halfway mark, as a samba band were playing next to the turnaround point. Naturally, we stopped for a dance and on the way back we were dishing out Love Hearts, a genius idea rustled up by my uni friend Clare.

I will never forget the feeling of completing that race. Partly because it was quite painful (not because of the running, but because I decided it would be fun for us to forward roll on the concrete surface over the finish line) but mostly because of the feeling of having completed a challenge in honour of Mum. Knowing that you have done something for someone you have lost and knowing, too, that by doing it you are helping a cause that is trying to prevent the same thing happening to others is overwhelmingly emotional. *This one's for you, Mum.*

Feeling tired but giddy, we kicked off our shoes and ran fully clothed into the sea for a cooldown, onlookers (quite understandably) bemused at what they were seeing. It was a fantastic day and, yet again, we had our closest friends around us to help us through it. My year, it seemed, was on the up.

Obviously, we had inspired some athletes around the world with our run, as the next month saw London proudly hosting the Olympics. Dad came up to London and we watched the Triathlon on the streets and on the big screen at Hyde Park, which was fantastic. I felt angry and frustrated that Mum was not able to see any of these amazing events. She should have been part of it. She lived a life of sport and would have loved to watch — but I tried to take it all in twice over, for her as well. I was determined to keep my spirits up.

As the Olympics were in their final stages, it was time for round two of bridesmaid duties. My school friend Beth was to be wed to Mat, who she had met when she and I worked for the same company in Bournemouth before my move to London. Mum knew Beth very well and I was so glad that she had heard about Beth's wedding before she died. She was so happy for her. I had not been very useful to Beth as a bridesmaid, given the year that I'd had, and I felt so guilty about this but, as one of my best friends, she completely understood. It was a big wedding for our school group — the first one! We all went down to Exeter and had the most incredible day. My clumsiness was responsible for a few slightly silly moments. I not only ripped Beth's dress a little with my heel (*I am so sorry*), but I also managed to spill my dinner down my own, which meant Beth and fellow brides-maid Charlotte ended up in the toilets with me to try to wash it out and dry it. When we got back to the Head Table, Beth was in stitches at the fact that someone had stolen my chair. 'Who steals a chair from the Head Table?' I kept shouting. *Seriously though?! More material for* Bridesmaids *2!*

What became very apparent at this wedding was that the words, 'till death us do part' will always break me. I will think of Mum and Dad every single time that I hear those words, because that is exactly what they did — they were there for each other until the end. Going to another wedding so soon also made me face up to the fact that my mum will never see my big day. *I can't begin to think about that.*

Just a month later in September — another month gone of trying our best to resume 'normal' life (*it will never be that again*) — yet another milestone was looming. This time it was poor Sarah's turn to face a birthday. It was a struggle for her and we made sure that we were all there, together as a family. The card is one of the hardest parts. We are so used to seeing our mum's name on it and, not only that, but seeing that familiar handwriting, too. Something that we had all found over the past months was that keeping busy was the best way to distract our minds from the fact Mum was not there. Sarah, Hannah, Joe and some of Sarah's friends and I spent the afternoon canoeing in Poole Bay. The only other time I had given this a go was years ago in France, when I had shared a canoe with Dad and Sarah. We had been the only ones in a group of many boats that had managed to get stuck on a rock. *I'm pretty sure that was my fault.* I was a little anxious about my second attempt on Sarah's birthday and I was right to be, as I was by far the worst canoer. Hey — at least I looked the part. *Oh wait — I'm wearing skinny jeans.* We took our soaked selves home for a change and some food and then headed out to Bournemouth for a drink and a dance. We had a lot of fun that day (which surprised us all) and Sarah had put on a brave face throughout. She did us proud once more.

October plodded along. I found that *I* was plodding along. The weddings, the Olympics — all of the positive events had shown me glimmers of hope — hope that I could still enjoy life. *I feel guilty being happy without her.* I was trying desperately hard to keep myself 'up' but my passion for most things had faded considerably. I felt like I was coasting at work — I was just trying to make it through the days. I consider myself a hard worker in anything that I do and I was all too aware that I was no longer giving it my all. I was in danger of giving up. I needed a new challenge.

A new challenge was offered to me through an exciting business trip. 'We need you to go to Singapore for three weeks. You would leave in two. Are you up for it?' asked my boss, Rob. 'Yes.' *Definitely, one hundred per cent — this has to happen.* Why would a business trip have such an effect on anything? It was because it was a three-week trip away from home in the same year that I had lost my mother and, while I was more than up for going on it, no matter how old you are you still want your mum to reassure you that you can do it. She was my main advisor. I was also very aware that I was going to be completely on my own out there and meeting new people. Although this year was looking up, would this bold adventure make me or break me? There was only one way to find out. *Flight booked.*

I was at Heathrow Airport and it wasn't a great start. I queued up to go through security. 'Madame you do know you can go to the fast track queue, don't you?' Clearly I did not, but I still said that I did and followed it up with asking where exactly it was. I went through to the Business Lounge and felt pretty uncomfortable, pretty quickly. I think that it was because I didn't look 'business' enough in my Primark jacket (£19.00 — *still available*).

When I was boarding, I tried my hardest to look cool as I walked through the plane towards my seat. I didn't look cool, though — I looked like a kid in a sweet shop. I faffed around for ages putting my bag, book and scarf in one place and then moving it to another. There were just so many options. *Lovely.*

It wasn't long before dinner was being served. 'Miss Chadwick, have you decided what you would like for your main yet?' I hadn't. And do you know why? It was because I had been completely distracted by the fact that I couldn't, for the life of me, figure out where the remote control was to work the TV. Fear not, I found its hiding place eventually. Oh and then I was served a five-course meal — absolutely delicious. *I will attempt to eat every last bite.*

I don't know if I was just overwhelmed by the experience, but I couldn't sleep at all. To fill my time I decided to watch not one, not two, not three — but four whole films. During this time I found myself red-faced with embarrassment when on not one occasion, but two, an air stewardess interrupted my viewing to ask if I needed anything just as a slightly risqué moment happened on the screen. *I must choose my films wisely on the return flight!*

When we landed I was surprised to feel more excited than nervous. As my taxi drove away from the airport to the city centre, we were heading towards high-rise heaven (*well, if you like that sort of thing*). Having little time to research Singapore before I got there, I knew they had a lot of tall buildings but I hadn't realised quite how many. (*I have googled it — there are fifty-nine to be precise.*) A positive that I took from the tall buildings was that I hoped it would make me feel a little bit smaller because, let's face it, next to the locals I was going to look gigantic — not ideal for the self-esteem. *I wish I was short — just like Mum.*

It was hot — so hot. It was humid, sweaty, muggy, but lovely. I don't want to complain about that like us Brits often do. The problem came when you walked *into* a building. In the words of my friend, say hello to 'aggressive air-conditioning'. He was absolutely right. When else have I needed an umbrella, mini-fan, scarf, flip-flops and big socks all in the space of five minutes?

As I wandered to work on my first day suffering from jet lag, I gazed at the business crowd in the Marina Bay area. It's got a City of London vibe but is just so much cooler (*don't get me wrong — it was still hot out*). Expats were all over the place, each of them trying to suss the other out with looks of 'What are you doing here?' 'Oh God, I have no idea,' said my sweaty face.

Unfortunately, I made quite the first impression at work. My colleagues had only known me for three hours when we got into the lift to go down for lunch. The jet lag was still right there with me. I leant against the wall in the lift and hit about ten floor buttons by accident. Oh, dear me. We then had to stop at every floor for the next ten. Everyone laughed hysterically every time the door opened. To try and make light of it, I told them that I'd done it on purpose as I was so keen to see what each floor looked like. More laughter followed, though this time it was definitely of the polite variety.

We were on our way to lunch when my colleagues asked me if there was anything in particular I disliked food-wise. *Black olives and raisins are probably not going to be an issue*. I told them I was game. I like a bit of spice and I will give most things a go. And so I did.

By lunch on day three, it became clear that I had been cast in a little play entitled 'How

Many Different Things Can We Make the English Girl Eat'? *So many*. There was something called *kway chap*, which was absolutely disgusting, but of course I smiled and nodded to be polite. The next morning, I found a team of very cheeky faces awaiting my arrival to the office. 'We can't believe you ate that yesterday!' *Ate what? Kway chap*, it transpired, was pig offal. No wonder it was so vile. When my team later asked what year I was born it made their day . . .

Getting the hang of chopsticks was pretty tricky — I was a classic for asking for a fork and a spoon in restaurants at home. One of my colleagues had even bought me some children's practice sticks to work with. *I fear this will be worse than asking for a spoon!* I tried and I tried and I splattered most of my food all over myself (*I swear my top was not that colour when I put it on in the morning? Ah yes — that will be the noodle juice*). But I finally got there — I would return to London and show off in the nearest Chinese restaurant.

Staying in a hotel on my own for the duration was refreshing at times and extremely lonely at others. Made more so by the time difference of eight hours. I got pretty confused, often messaging people to ask if they were around to find that they were working, or worse — sleeping. *Hello there — anyone want to chat? Hello?* So much alone time, as predicted, allowed me a lot of time to think about Mum. So much had happened since she had passed and now I was in another continent wishing that I could tell her all about it. Still, I had a library of DVDs to browse and a gym and pool to hit to distract me from spiralling into a dark state.

While I was there, one of my best friends Clare came to see me for the weekend. She flew over from Brunei where she had been living for the past five years with her husband. It was amazing to see her. Of all of my friends, she was the one who knew Mum the best. She had grown up with me — she went to Dad's tennis coaching and attended the same dancing school so we spent a huge amount of time together. Clare became a friend of the family, often calling Mum her 'second mum'. This meant that I could totally relax around her and talk about Mum freely. It was so refreshing — such a good thing for me. *I can talk about her to my heart's content.* I left our reunion feeling happy but sad at the same time, as I realised it would be such a long time before I could see Clare again.

Everyone I met in Singapore was so welcoming and I felt like I was fitting in well.

I had been so anxious about this trip, even suffering from mild panic attacks before leaving the UK. I work myself up into a frenzy and it causes my body to completely break down on me. I had suffered from a few since Mum passed and I sincerely hoped they would go away. Singapore was turning out to be a great experience for me, though, and I really felt like I was getting my confidence back. The vibe may be chilled, but their work ethic is very strong. Even though I had lost a lot of passion for work and for life when I lost Mum, this place seemed to be bringing me back up. It was amazing to be thrown into the deep end and, despite the fact that I thought about Mum a lot, I enjoyed having my space and being faced with a new challenge. *I don't want to forget this feeling.*

On my return to London I was in good spirits, until I realised that it was my birthday coming up — the next milestone on the list. *Thank goodness I was just the right side of thirty — don't want to have to worry about that on top of everything else.* Given that these constant date reminders were wearing me down, I probably should have kept this birthday chilled. But no, I booked a bar and invited about fifty people. *Good one.*

When I woke up on my birthday morning to a breakfast my housemates had made for me, I couldn't hold back the tears. My first birthday without my mum around and, boy, did I feel it. I started to regret the party I had planned for that weekend. At least I had a lovely day in central London with my family to look forward to. We met at Embankment and went to have coffee at Café Rouge just up the street, and I was so excited when they gave me a new camera. I had no idea! Photography was on my list of things to do and this camera was going to come in useful for the next trip abroad I took. It was a trip that I had been thinking about for a while. It was time for the city break with a twist. It was time for my postcard adventure in Paris — my tribute to my mother.

6

My Tribute

When my mum was first diagnosed with cancer I started to think about all of the things that I wanted to do with her. I was bursting to tell the world about Mum, especially as there were so many moments when I felt that I couldn't. Sometimes it was too tough for me to bring her up at all but, when I desperately wanted to, I found there was rarely a social situation where chatting about my loss would be acceptable. Death is such a frightfully taboo topic — it shouldn't be, but it is. I wanted an opportunity to change that. It was time to speak up. *Loudly*.

I had spent the months since my mother's death in somewhat of a blur and I had been trying my best to cope with the grief — putting on a brave face to the world — as, behind closed doors, my world was crashing in around me. I couldn't see a way out of the dark place that I had fallen into — I was being pulled further down by every single milestone that I was forced to face. Every time that I started to pick myself up — I was dragged down by another one. It was a roller coaster of grief. And another milestone was coming up. Mum's sixtieth birthday loomed on the horizon. But then it dawned on me — rather than waiting anxiously for another day of misery, why don't I try to do something completely different? My mum was not given a chance to fight so, in her honour, I was going to step up and give grief the battle of its life. *Bring it on*. I would go on an anniversary trip that would put every other weekend away to shame. I wanted to do something fun, something distinctive and, more than anything, something totally unique in memory of this extraordinary lady in my life. This was my chance to leave a long-lasting tribute for a woman who could not deserve it more.

My mum was my everything. *She still is my everything*. She was such an inspiring woman, passionate about everything that she did and so kind and caring. She taught me that being a people person in life means so much — to treat others as you would expect to be treated. She was everything I could wish to be in a woman. I know that we would have done something special for her sixtieth. I wanted to make sure that still happened, despite the tragic fact that she was no longer with us. I would celebrate for her in her honour in the most imaginative and creative way I could think of. I would leave a long-lasting memory of such a deserved human being. It was the least that I could do.

I was wracking my brain about how this tribute could be documented. Writing is an old passion of mine which all stemmed from school. I adored my English lessons — it was my favourite subject by far, which led me to study for a degree in English Language at Cardiff University. I always felt so sure that I would continue writing, even if it was only in my spare time. But sometime, somehow — the spark faded.

When I first moved to London in October 2008, my housemate at the time, Rachel, began to pester me to start a blog. We used to send each other witty emails, but mainly she thought I should do it because ridiculous stories seemed to come out of my day-to-day life. But I just didn't feel it was enough — it seemed too self-indulgent and without any depth or real purpose to write about how I had fallen down some stairs or sent a text message to the wrong person. And so, I put writing and, with it, my passion on the back burner once more.

But now this was about to change. A blog would be the perfect platform to write about both the memorial project and to jot down all of the words, feelings and memories whirling around in my head about Mum. I finally had a strong and heartfelt purpose behind my writing. I finally had something and someone to do this for. A blog it would be.

Rather than going solo, I emailed my closest friends with an invitation to join me on an anniversary weekend. I wondered about how to phrase it — I did not want the fact that it was such a personal journey to make them feel pressured into coming. On the other hand, they are my closest friends — I should be honest about my reasoning behind the trip. It was hugely important to me and I couldn't spring it on them when they arrived. I said that I would be going in memory of Mum's sixtieth and a flurry of 'I'm in' responses cluttered my inbox. They would be right there by my side. *Amazing.* I have always been grateful for the friends that I have in my life but it was at this moment that it really hit me just how incredible they are. *I am a lucky girl.*

Why did I choose Paris? Well, there were never any other contenders. The last gift my mum had given me was the Eurostar vouchers for my twenty-eighth birthday — the last birthday of mine that she shared with me. She had chosen them especially because she knew how much I desperately wanted to visit The City of Love. Not only that, but 'Love' was Mum's maiden name. *Now that is a fact far too fitting to ignore!* The word 'Love' gained a whole new meaning the minute that my mother passed away. Every time I see it written down, it makes me think about her and I think about that 'Love' sign that she bought on the Southbank on her last visit to London. She was so proud of her family name, and I was too. *I wish she had double-barrelled — no offence to Dad, of course.*

I wanted to leave a message about Mum in Paris explaining why I was there — perhaps Love Hearts, Post-its or something written on stickers? *No, stickers won't work. I don't want to deface the place.* It was actually on a trip home to Dorset during a coffee with Hannah in a little café called Cloisters, where we had spent many an afternoon having a cuppa and a cream tea with Mum, that she helped me come up with the idea of postcards. *Postcards!* Tourists are forever sending postcards home from their trips abroad. They hold such a personal message for all to see with no envelope to hide it. Rather than sending postcards home of my experiences, I was going to use them in the opposite way — to tell the people in the city I was visiting exactly why I was there. This was the perfect way to leave my message about Mum.

'60 Postcards in Paris' had a lovely ring to it, too. *Lightning strikes!* I would scatter postcards around the city — one postcard to celebrate every year of my mother's life. *This* would be my creative project. But I couldn't help but feel that there was something missing. I think it was my passion for meeting new people (it is one of my favourite pastimes) that gave me the idea. What if I left my details on each postcard in case someone found it and wanted to get in touch? Was that a little too bonkers? Imagine if I actually heard back from someone, though? It was a long shot, it was a risk, but I was willing to give anything a go. I had absolutely nothing to lose. (Apart from my sanity, which I think was on its way out anyway!)

I bought sixty postcards the week before the trip, plus a few spares thrown in (*the land of* vin rouge = *mistakes*). I chose the cards with the most Parisian feel to them. Ironic, really, that I bought them from Paperchase, one of my regular drop-in shops in King's Cross Station. Oh, and the poor shop assistant at the time. 'I'm sorry but I have to scan these in one by one,' he sighed. It wasn't me he needed to apologise to — it was the increasing number of people waiting patiently (or not so) behind me!

So, getting the postcards was the easy bit. Now for the hard part — the words. What did I write? OK, so, the brief was to keep it short. I wanted to write the same message on every single postcard so that there was some consistency. If I wrote a different thing on each one, I would wonder if the message was affecting whether anyone would respond. This way I would be leaving the same imprint in sixty different places around Paris. The tricky part was working out how I was going to get everything I needed to say in such a small space, while providing the reader with enough information to understand exactly what I was doing and why.

And, of course, I had to be certain that my email address was legible (kudos to Trent for pointing out that one — he became the quality control master). After a bit (OK — a lot) of trial and error, the following words were chosen to be the message written on each of the postcards:

LIS S'IL VOUS PLAIT! PLEASE READ!
Bonjour/Hello!
I'm Rachael from London, visiting Paris with my friends for the weekend in memory of my mother who passed away in February. To

117

remember her and to celebrate her 60th birthday,
I am leaving 60 postcards around Paris. I am
going to document this weekend in a blog and I
would love you to be part of it. Please email me
with your name and a little story about what
you were doing when you found this! Please feel
free to leave it for someone else to find!
Thank you / Merci!
Rachael xxx
(*Email address*)

Why did I choose the old-school handwritten
approach? I like old school. As an eighties
child (I've got love for you, too, Calvin
Harris), I grew up doing all of my schoolwork
putting pen to paper. (Until we hit sixth form
and those computer machines both terrified
me and blew my mind — once you had
waited half an hour for the Internet to
connect. Oh, how I miss that sound.) The
world of social media is taking over, not
slowly but definitely surely, and I wanted to
go back to basics and leave something a lot
more authentic. Something printed would be
far less likely to be noticed — I know I would
be more drawn to a handwritten note than a
typed one. It is so much more personal. *I*
would definitely pick one up! And I still love
to write things down by hand, especially lists
(*my favourite*). One of the many things

handed down to me from my mother — she was a list fanatic and took a huge amount of pride in her catalogue of pretty notebooks. You've got to appreciate a good to-do list. So, why did I leave my email address and not my home address? It is true that, if I had done, people could have posted the cards back but giving my home address to complete strangers seemed a (crazy) step (far) too far. Not that I imagine anyone would have turned up at my house, but it really wasn't worth the risk. So I would use the twenty-first century to my advantage, in spite of my aforesaid admiration for the written note. Also, the age of the smart phone is upon us and with them come very good cameras (not to mention being able to 'Instagram the beep out of them' — a phrase used by myself and many a friend). If anyone found my postcard with one of these smarty-pants phones then they could take a snap right there and then and could even email me from the spot, too, or at least make a note of my email address. That way they could leave the postcard where they found it. *It is all falling into place!*

Now, this explanation makes it sound as if I had really thought all of this through for weeks, months even, before we left. But it actually came about very quickly during brainstorming sessions (my father tells me that 'mind showers' is the new phrase for that) with friends and family. You see, a more organised person would have pre-written all sixty postcards before the trip. Did I? Nope. 'Organised' isn't exactly one of the five words I would use to describe myself. *It's really not my style.* I'm more, how should I put it? 'Lastminute.com'. To be fair (*I say to make myself feel better*), I had just got back from my business trip in Singapore and I was rushed off my feet. *Excuses, excuses.* Besides, writing them in Paris meant I had the help of the Paris Crew, as I called them. It could be a team-bonding experience (which admittedly they had not been pre-warned about). We could write them together as we explored Paris. It would add to the fun factor. *A beautiful plan is created from very little planning at all.*

But where would I leave the messages? It was a conscious decision not to make a set list (*even though, as you know, I do love lists*). I had never been to the city before, there were twelve of us to navigate around and we couldn't be sure how much ground we would be able to cover in just three days. With such a loose itinerary (almost non-existent, in fact), I thought it would be best to play it by ear (*or 'p.i.b.e.' it, as I like to say*). We could distribute them as we went

— picking the places and moments that felt right at the time. *Note: it really must feel 'right' — I don't want to waste one postcard.*

So I would scatter the city with her memory to celebrate her birthday in style. This was me reaching out to the people of Paris — to the locals and tourists — to see if they would answer my call. If they did, I would be in contact with someone new — perhaps they would become a friend? Even if I never heard from anyone at all, I would have celebrated Mum's birthday with my closest friends in a unique and exciting way — I had to give it a try. And knowing how creative my mum was, there was no doubt that this was a tribute she would have loved to hear about.

60 Postcards had been born. This would be my gift, my tribute and my legacy for Mum.

7

The City of Love

We awoke on tribute weekend after our first night's sleep in our perfectly Parisian apartment — all in our separate rooms, shouting, 'Morning!' sleepily through the walls to each other. It was our first day to explore the city as a group. The fun was really about to begin.

I had slept in a bed with my housemate, Katie. As we lay trying to stir from our sleepy daze, I reminded her of a conversation we'd had at three o'clock in the morning. I had awoken in a chill as I realised that my good friend had, unintentionally, stolen all of the covers and had left me shivering. *Ahem — I'm FREEZING*. I nudged Katie gently, scared to frighten her. I asked her if she could hand me back some of the covers and she gave me the most polite response that I could imagine (I would have been fuming to be woken at that ungodly hour). She muttered, 'Oh, Rachael, I am so sorry. I *must* not do this,' in a very posh accent. I was chuckling to

122

myself as I tried to go back to sleep, imagining what she must have been dreaming about to come out with such a voice — perhaps she was a member of the *Made in Chelsea* cast? *Spencer was up to no good again, probably.* Even more amusing was that she had no recollection of the conversation!

Katie, Bethan and I were the first up and ready (which was surprising for me), and so we decided to brave the wintery morning air and do the bread run. I took some postcards with me in my bag (deciding it would be best to carry them at all times) and we stopped off for a latte just around the corner from the apartment. Bethan and Katie read their books as I set out to write my message, which I noticed I was beginning to know off by heart. *My hand is already aching. This doesn't bode well — I have so many more to do!* The *boulangerie* that we went into just opposite the café was a joy to behold. The smell of freshly made bread filled the air — Bethan was in heaven. Bethan has a serious love for all things doughy (and, not to mention, cheesy) and it soon became a joke of the trip, as we would tease her every time we passed any delicatessen. *Here she goes!*

We took the baguettes, warm croissants and pastries back to, what felt like, our new home. We set the table for breakfast, complete with orange juice and hot coffee, as the Paris Crew (as they were known to me) were getting showered upstairs. They filtered down one by one as we took it in turns to delve into the breakfast delights. As I stared at the table, I began to pull at the waistband of my jeans. If this was going to be our staple diet for the trip (which it most definitely was), then I was going to have to do some serious exercise on my return home. But, hang on — it would be almost Christmas when we got back. I would have to add 'exercise' to the growing list of New Year's resolutions instead. *It's going to be a busy year.*

While the others were getting ready, I was delighted to answer the door to my best friend, Caroline, who had come over on the Eurostar that morning to join the gang. We were now an eleven-strong group. *This will be an experience!* It took a good couple of hours, in the end, for everyone to be washed, dressed, fed and watered before we gathered in the huge living space. We wrapped ourselves up in our coats, gloves and scarves, not to mention the double socks, and were finally ready to set off for the day. *We are ready for you, Paris.*

I looked around the room and felt incredibly lucky to have so many people there to support me for this weekend. I had met them all at different times in my life and I was excited that they would be able to get to know each other better. It is always a little daunting bringing a group of friends together — but I knew that this lot were bound to get on like a house on fire.

First up there was Beth. She is the friend that I have known the longest. We met at playgroup at the age of three, attended First School together and met again at High School. Beth and I played a lot of tennis together growing up and I had the pleasure of being her bridesmaid. She now lives in Exeter and I always wish that she was a little bit closer to me.

Amy and I have been buddies since we attended Allenbourn Middle School (where Mum taught). Amy and I were the only ones from our gang of school friends who were living in Dorset during one particular year after university and this was when our friendship became stronger than ever. Amy is a great influence on me on the culture front, often taking me to the Soho Theatre to see the latest play or comedy.

Bethan, 'The Bread Lover', is another friend from Middle School. It was our love of all things sporty (including wearing tracksuits in our social hours — *cringe*) that brought us together and this girl is the very reason that I first moved to London. She convinced me to take the spare room in her flat that was about to become available. I am so glad I made that move! It only takes a few minutes together for Bethan and I to find that our voices and gestures are totally in sync!

Housemate Beccy and I met when I first moved to London. She is the best lady to dance with in the kitchen and is a total film guru, always showing me the best on screen. With her strong passion for film, I look forward to attending the Oscars as her guest in the future.

I met Caroline when I started working in London about five years ago and we clicked immediately. So much so, that I called my mum that evening to tell her about my new London friend. Caroline has so many strings to her bow she is almost a walking orchestra. On top of her full-time job, Caroline acts, sings in a band and is often found drinking wine in bars with me as we people watch and list write. *We need to get shares in Café Boheme.*

Welsh girl Clare came into my life through playing netball together at uni. She teaches and lives in London and is such a do-er (so to speak) — theatre, rollerskating, circus skills training — you name it and she's done it. And I don't think I have ever met anyone who excels at fancy dress as much as this girl. She has the nickname 'Fun Clare' because that is exactly what she is.

I met Geordie boy David when Clare brought him along one weekend — they used to work in the same school together. I think even at our first meeting he demonstrated that he was not only an incredible mover on the dance floor, but that he also loves to sing. *He takes requests.*

Katie was my housemate until very recently. Earlier this year, she flew off to Brazil to work out there for two years. Otherwise known as 'Kazzle', this girl is hot on languages and has a love for all things Latin. She pretends that she is not very good at French but that is a lie. *Elle est très bonne! (Is that right?!)*

Kerry (the one crew member still to arrive) went to college with Katie and it's hard to believe I've only known her a couple of years — it feels like far longer. We've already been on trips to Croatia, Paris (of course) and even Cardiff (*my uni city — I heart that place*). Kerry is a cheeky one and we always have fun being sarccy with each other and putting the world to rights over a glass of wine.

Stew and I met at High School. Like Katie, Stew is excellent at languages and he always finds much amusement in trying to teach me (often rude phrases — not that I know!). Oh, and the way this man can tell a story is pure magic — I could listen to him chat all night!

Trent is my third and final housemate and I adore living with him. He is super-smart and witty and, although he won't believe me, I find his laugh endearing and infectious. Trent is a very talented writer and also a great advisor to me. He is simply a wondrous man.

The Paris Crew had decided to head for La Basilique du Sacré-Coeur on Montmartre Hill for our first expedition. Hopping on the Métro would cut out too much scenery, though. We were there to see as much as possible and we were so used to being underground in London we wanted to see the light of day! So we set off on foot. Walking turned into strolling, which turned into grinding halts. 'Wait! Stewart has gone to get gloves.' 'Who wants a crêpe? Should we get a crêpe yet? I think I fancy a crêpe.' Funnily enough, it was Bethan who fancied a crêpe. (*I must add at this point that, even though I keep mentioning her stuffing her face, Bethan is very sporty and slender!*)

It felt a little like herding cattle with eleven of us trying to get from one place to another. Not that I know what that is like, despite what some people in London think when they find out my hometown is in Dorset (*I do not have a farm — E-I-E-I-O).*

I felt a little stressed about the fact that everything was going to take so much longer than expected. Should I have brought an umbrella to hold in the air — the classic move of the leader of a tourist pack? I told myself to get over it and chill out. As we all wandered along, grinding to a halt once again, I suddenly realised where we were. We had finally made it to a lovely road in Montmartre called rue Lepic. It was time to take a well-deserved, leisurely pit stop at a café. We'd had a coffee or two at the apartment so the next most obvious option was a Kir Royale (*oh, so obvious*). Sitting at the tables outside, we nattered and soaked up the Saturday afternoon sunshine and, not to mention, the buzz of the area. This place was people-watching heaven. Mum would have loved it — it was one of her favourite pastimes. I almost felt French sitting there sipping my drink. The only problem was I can barely speak the language. *Je suis désolé.*

I felt like I was on a film set, though. Oh, wait a minute. That was because this very place had actually been a film set. This was no ordinary café — this was the *Amélie* café, the Café des Deux Moulins. It looked exactly the same as it does in the film. It suddenly dawned on me that the storyline of *Amélie* was actually somewhat similar to what I was doing and I hadn't even realised when I came up with the project. *Get with the picture — literally.* Leaving notes for someone to find — of course! I made a mental note to watch the film again as soon as I was home.

I suddenly felt extremely nervous. Why? Because I knew — I knew, as we were about to leave the café, that this was it; this was the first moment. It was time to leave a postcard. I waited for everyone else to get a head start and then I placed one on the table. I turned on my heels and walked away as quickly as I could. *This is strange — was I being too obvious?* I found it difficult to resist the urge to look back. *Don't do it!* It may have felt odd but I had butterflies in my stomach and excitement in my heart as I wondered if this plan would ever work. Would anyone find the postcard? And would they respond even if they did? *Everything is crossed!*

I sped up the hill to catch up with the others. I was trying to contain my new-found, nervous excitement. *This is going to be a lot of fun!* We only got as far as the end of the road before we stopped yet again. HALT! It was another *boulangerie* that left our mouths watering as we stared at the delicious goods through the glass window. We had to drag Bethan away!

The hill was getting steeper and we slowed down our pace and took a look at the windmill halfway up where there was a photo shoot going on with a faux bride and groom. This was a perfect Kodak moment — out came the camera. I thought back to my 'to-do' list — photography — I was finally ticking something off, at least! It made it even more enjoyable to know that it was something my mum encouraged me to do. This whole trip was in celebration of her — I wanted to make the most of this special weekend.

We weaved in and out of winding cobbled roads and came around a corner to find that we had lost some of the gang in the space of just five minutes. Beccy, Trent, Clare, David, Caroline and I came across some buskers playing outside a gorgeous little art gallery. One man was on his guitar and another man with a very fetching woolly panda hat was banging a wooden board for percussion. *I need one of those in my life.* We stopped to listen and found ourselves starting to sway, shoulder dancing and foot tapping along to the music. We got so into it that we started cheering loudly, which seemed to be drawing more and more fellow tourists to join the audience. Before long the buskers had a very large crowd blocking the road in front of them. *The traffic can wait — this is a big gig.*

The shoulder dancing soon progressed to what can only be described as crazies dancing in the street. I gave them some coins and slipped a postcard into the box, too. As I walked back to my friends I couldn't help but raise my hands and sway along, lost in the moment. But we didn't stop there. Others may have done, but us lot? We'd lost the plot (*years ago*). Beccy and Trent, my wonderful housemates, took to the stage as backing dancers, free-styling with improvised choreography. I recognised some of the moves from our kitchen dancing at home. *Classic shapes*. It was at this point that I couldn't speak for crying so much — tears of uncontrollable laughter.

The song was infectious — their passion for music was infectious. The tune at the time featured a lot of, 'AY, AY, AY' in the chorus. What made us laugh even more was that the buskers were so pleased about the growing crowd (*anyone would think it was Wembley Arena*) that they decided to do an extended version of the song. Somehow ten minutes later we still seemed to be singing 'AY, AY, AY'. It was the longest encore I have ever experienced — neither the performers nor the audience wanted this moment to end! Keen to have a memory of that experience, I bought their album. Ten euros well spent.

When we finally left the buskers behind, it took us a while to stop bopping along as we wandered off. *What a day so far.*

We found the rest of our gang on the steps of the Basilica at the top of Montmartre Hill and told them the tale of our musical moment, while we enjoyed a well-earned mulled wine and admired the incredible view across the whole of the city below us.

Entertainment part *deux* of the day came at the bottom of the steps where a man had climbed up a lamp post while doing football tricks and balancing circus-style, all at the same time. He was such a talent and after a bit of Google action, one of the gang informed us that he had been on the French version of *Britain's Got Talent*. (Which is probably called *France's Got Talent* — but in French!) *Je ne sais pas.*

Stomachs were beginning to grumble. We had only covered about thirty minutes of ground by foot, but as a group of eleven with wine stops, crêpe breaks, postcard dropping and dancing with buskers — time had flown by and it was already early afternoon! It was time for a late lunch. We had a big night out planned for that evening and I could almost hear my mother in my head, ordering me to line my stomach! So, off we went marching back up the stairs to the Basilique, while

David kicked off a rendition of Mariah's All I Want for Christmas is You. We all joined in for the chorus as tourists around us listened on amused (or possibly horrified). We were street entertainers ourselves, just with a little (*a lot*) less talent.

Now the tricky thing about lunch was going to be finding somewhere that could take eleven people. *Good luck, Paris.* We had all rehearsed saying, '*Nous sommes onze*' and had also prepared ourselves for the shocked faces that would be the response. We walked back down the hill and found the perfect restaurant with a long table upstairs that seemed to have been made just for us. *Perfect.* Let the private party commence. We ordered all sorts of foods and I knew we were looking at a long stay here, especially as we started to order wine to go with it. We did a huge '*Salut*'. Life was good. I was feeling very good — probably the best that I had felt all year. I had my friends around me and I had postcards to be scattered for my mum.

On the slow walk back to the apartment to get ready for our night out, someone (naming no names because there were so many of us I can't be sure who the culprit was) thought it would be a good idea to drop into a bar to do a shot of tequila or sambuca. *Uh oh!* I felt extremely grateful that I had eaten so much bread along with my meal. Down the hatch it went and we continued on. As we wandered home we admired the Moulin Rouge that was all lit up and I thought about the film — my mum loved that film. She loved to sing Your Song. It was a happy memory and one that only a couple of months ago would have brought me to tears. But I was feeling stronger than ever on this trip. I felt more like myself than I had done for months.

It wouldn't have been right, in this part of town, if we hadn't taken a little look in a sex shop. Picture this — eleven people in their late twenties walk in and eleven giggling teenagers walk out. We just couldn't help it. And perhaps the cheeky shot hadn't helped. I left a postcard inside. I didn't hold up much hope of receiving replies as it was — let alone from there — but, still, it was worth a go! I had begun to leave more as I went along during the day, growing in confidence. It felt strange — I was sneaking around like a thief. But I wasn't stealing anything, I was leaving something behind. It reminded me of something Caroline had said to me, 'reverse robber'. I like that — I like that a lot.

On arrival back at the apartment it was time for a pre-drinking, getting-ready session. We put some tunes on, including the buskers' CD, of course — which we realised did not have quite the same effect as it had when we were dancing in the street! We cracked open the wine and laid out the cheese and bread (we would need that for stamina — we all loved a good dance). It was going to be a fight for the showers but, as I am known to be one of the last to be ready, no one complained about me getting in there first. We were all getting glammed up for tonight. I put some curls in my hair and some red lippy on (*when in Paris*) and got into my new black dress, feeling the most Parisienne chic I think I will ever come close to. Then it was back to the sunken area for a glass of wine and a boogie to the music. The cameras were out and we were all trying to get pictures of each other, which we then spent a further half an hour trying to Instagram to make us look as good as possible. *How did we ever survive with throw-away cameras?*

We congregated in the kitchen area when we were all dolled up, laughing at Clare and David who had decided it would be a good idea to give David's hair a cut with the blunt kitchen scissors while under the influence of alcohol. *Don't try this at home!* Bethan had us all in stitches as she seemed to have found a new love for the word 'Regardez!', which was frequently used from then on, whether in or out of context.

We finished off our drinks and went out into the cold night to grab some taxis. We were heading for a bridge on the Seine. That sounds like an odd night out but Stewart had lived in Paris and he knew a club called Showcase that he thought would be perfect for us. As we pulled up in the taxi we could see the Eiffel Tower lit up in all its glory in the distance. This was the closest that we had come to it so far. *I feel more in Paris than ever!* We got to the Alexandre III Bridge and walked down the slope and around the corner below it to enter the club. We felt like a bunch of seventeen-year-olds as we realised they were asking everyone that entered for identification. The school friends of mine and I looked at each other knowingly. *We've been in this situation before.* Most of us didn't have any identification with us — we only had our passports in Paris and bringing them on a night out drinking was an absolute no. *Mine will end up in the Seine.* Should we get Stewart or Katie to speak to them in French? No, let's play the we-are-not-from-here card. It worked. Well, either that or it was glaringly obvious that we were all in our late twenties. Still — we had made it into the club.

It was a very cool underground space with stone walls and colourful lighting. We headed to a bar on the left and took it in turns to order some drinks. *Très expensive! Ah, we're on holiday after all!* They sold test-tube shots. We laughed at how these tourist haunts go for the novelty factor and then continued to purchase a round of them. *It works.* After we had enjoyed our drinks it was time to hit the dance floor to make some shapes. It was bar, dance floor and repeat for the next few hours and we had a great time. Beth even bumped into someone she knew from Exeter who ended up joining the group for a while and Clare announced that she knew someone in there, too! Clearly this was the place to be on a Saturday night out in the city. It seemed more for the younger crowd but, still, we had given them a run for their money with our shapes. (*I keep saying shapes — young people don't say 'shapes'.*)

When it was time to depart we got a little separated, as we needed to get three taxis. Some of us got back to the flat earlier than others and, as we were a little hungry, we decided to get stuck into a midnight snack — *OK, feast.* We munched away to our hearts' content, not realising quite how much of the leftovers we had polished off. Clare was on the sofa when the rest of the gang came in and she told me later that she had to try so hard not to laugh, pretending that she was asleep, as she started to hear, '*Où est le pain?*'

shouted repeatedly as the poor guys who were last in were left with absolutely nothing.

Sunday morning was a struggle. *These hangovers get tougher every single time.* As we were all feeling more than a little worse for wear, it was going to take a lot to get us moving. I was so tired, not only because of the late night, but also from that awfully early start on Friday for the journey to Paris (*still milking it*). There was no way that I was going to make the bread run this morning. I hoped that someone in a better state than me would be getting the *pain* on the table soon!

I finally woke up properly and literally leaped out of bed as I remembered what was happening that morning. We had our final Paris Crew member arriving. Kerry texted me from the Gare du Nord to let me know that she was on her way to the apartment. *Nice one! The party will be complete.* The best thing about Kerry arriving was that Katie had no idea. I had been in email conversation not long before the trip with Kerry when she had told me that, after thinking she would have to miss out, she had an opportunity to join us at the last minute. As Kerry and Katie are best friends, I thought it would be a lovely surprise for her, so everyone had kept it quiet. When Kerry came to the door, I answered it — making sure that Katie was in the room. Well, I am not sure I have ever seen such a late reaction. Katie stared for a while and then suddenly let out a high-pitched laugh. She looked around at everyone as if to say, 'Look — it's Kerry.' She had no idea we were all in on it. When they gave each other a huge hug, I felt very happy that the surprise had gone to plan. We were now a gang of twelve. '*Nous sommes douze!*'

The destination that we were aiming for that morning was the Champs-Élysées. As our suffering bodies were slower than ever, there was no hope of us all being ready at the same time — not unless we planned on leaving in the afternoon! The sunken area may be good, but it wasn't where we should be spending the whole of our Sunday while there were still so many sights waiting for us out there.

Some of us chose to walk and that included me. I love wandering. I will forever choose a wander over a tube. I was so enjoying walking around the pretty streets of Paris imagining that I was a local (who had simply lost her voice). It was just as I had hoped it would be and more. We hadn't even come to the end of the trip yet and I was already so excited at the prospect of coming back again in the future. *I am such a nightmare for that. Sometimes I* even get holiday blues before I have left home — just the thought of having to come back at the end! As we had all gone off separately, I made sure that everyone was armed with a couple of postcards each — just in case an opportunity arose — and I left a couple in postcard racks on the way down to the river, passing boutiques, a million cafés and a fair few chocolate shops to keep us happy.

The Champs-Élysées was brimming with Christmas joy when we got there. White market stalls went on for what seemed like miles and they were all showered with festive decorations. We found a mulled wine stall, not simply because we wanted a drink, but the cold was making our hands numb, even through our gloves. *I cannot feel my fingers. Do I still have any?* When people told me that Paris would be freezing at this time of year, I shrugged it off. *Hey, I am from England — I know what cold feels like.* But I should have listened — I felt like I had icicles hanging off my nose.

We wandered down looking at the stalls and it made me think of the Southbank and my birthday the year before. The Southbank always reminds me of Mum so much, especially now, as it was the last time I had seen her in London. And it was in that instant that I realised I hadn't had one dark moment about Mum since we'd arrived in Paris. No sad time. The only tears that I had cried were ones of laughter. I realised that this trip, turning something into a celebration, was helping more than ever. *Everything seems a little lighter.*

We got to the gates at the entrance of the Jardin des Tuileries and I stuck a postcard in between the railings, hoping that it wouldn't fall out and trying to make sure the words were visible — it was a tricky job placing these postcards. We wandered in, all of us walking at different paces, people chatting among themselves, and I noticed that everyone was getting on so well. My master plan had worked — just as I had predicted they were getting on like a house on fire.

When we reached the Louvre I took about two shots before my camera went blank. The batteries had died. *I've overdone it.* To be honest, this was good timing — I loved being part of a big group but it would be nice to go off on my own for a little while to try and find some replacements for my camera and have a bit of much-needed 'me' time. I wasn't in any rush to find a shop and wandered aimlessly for a while before I happened upon a souvenir shop with music blasting out. I walked in to find the two staff dancing to 'Gangnam Style'! Naturally I joined in and I suddenly wished that someone had been there to experience it with me. *Look how crazy these people are. Brilliant.* I bought my batteries from this comedy duo and called Sarah, my sister, for a chat on the way back to the Louvre. I told her all about the adventures so far and insisted that we go to Paris together at some point.

Walking past the Louvre on my own meant that I kept being stopped to take photographs for people. *They are probably drawn by my new camera.* It must have happened about five times in the space of five minutes! I had to get my head down and get out of there quickly. *Don't make eye contact.* The rest of the Paris Crew had found warmth in the Café du Thé just beyond the Louvre and I found them all sipping their cappuccinos as Katie had the huge map of the city out on the table in front of her, planning our next move. It was at this point that we had to say goodbye to Clare and David — they had to get back as they were teaching the next day. It was the end of a Paris Crew era! *Nous sommes douze* no more.

The rest of us walked from the café across the river and down to Saint-Germain-des-Prés. I fell in love with the place immediately — designer shops, posh bars and gorgeous Parisian people. *Why did I wear this outfit?* I wondered if, perhaps, I could move here. *If only*. That would be a good way to get myself speaking French. I had been trying the lingo but I found it more difficult than I imagined. Good job I had Stewart there to lead the way (or lead me astray with his cheeky phrases!).

We found the perfect restaurant with classic French food and a big table at the back of the room for lunch, which looked like it had been laid out especially for us. The waiter was so friendly and we couldn't help but notice the bar men were quite easy on the eye. Yes — this would do nicely.

For some strange reason, even though it was only late afternoon, we were given glow sticks with our drinks. For a moment I thought we might be in Ayia Napa! No, no — we were still in Paris. We wore our glow sticks as a way of thanks to the staff. (*Oh no, they probably think we are on an episode of* Brits Abroad. *Horrendous.*) We even got a smiley face drawn on our receipt. I drew one back, of course. This had been a very random but enjoyable lunch — I would definitely return there (if I could find it again). I left a postcard on my seat as we got up. I was beginning to be braver with the postcards, leaving them in more places — telephone boxes, photo booths, café tables, on notice-boards and in little nooks and crannies.

Doing it was becoming natural to me. I wondered if I should leave postcards everywhere I go in life!

My phone beeped and it was a message from Clare. It said that there may be some kind of problem with the apartment — Antoinette had gone in to see them and had asked if they were the last to leave as the cleaner was coming in. Uh oh — had I not booked for Sunday night? This would be funny (if nine of us being stranded in the cold could be seen as funny). I called Antoinette and, thankfully, it had just been a misunderstanding. I breathed a sigh of relief. I wouldn't have been the most popular girl in the world if that had happened. Clare and David had decided that it only classed as a 'mild to mid panic' that we would be homeless, though, so, once she had sent the text message to me, they hoped for the best, nailed a bottle of wine to relax and then rushed to the airport. On getting there they had found that they had no clue where their terminal was and almost missed their flight. *That is exactly the kind of thing that I would do!*

It was soon time for another crew member to leave us — time to say goodbye to Bethan. As afternoon turned into evening, the rest of us went to Le Marais for a drink. We found a bar and all ordered our drinks and gathered around a group of tables outside. It didn't take long for us to get the feeling the bar staff didn't like us. It was probably something to do with the fact that we were a huge group in a tiny gay bar. Feeling a little disgruntled, we headed to another bar in honour of Katie and her love for all things Latin. It was called, Barrio. Katie and I had spent so many nights in the Barrio in Soho we thought it would only be right to try out the Parisian version.

As it was a Sunday night it was pretty quiet but we found ourselves in a Moroccan-styled room and we all sat around and talked about the tales of the trip so far over yet another *vin rouge*. Suddenly the music was turned up and there were a few more people flowing in. Beccy, Katie and Kerry couldn't resist getting up for a dance. I was usually one of the first ones up but I felt a little tired and obviously the blues were setting in about home time tomorrow. *How can I stop these premature holiday blues?*

As we got back to La Fourche Métro station, we decided to go to a little roadside *crêperie*. There were quite a few of us to be fed but crêpes wouldn't take long, we thought. This would have been true had we not happened upon the most chilled-out crêpe man in the whole of Paris. I took one for the team and agreed to go last as the others wandered back to the house to devour their crêpes and hit the sack. *I am so jealous — I can barely keep my eyes open.* By the time I made it back from that place, some people had probably had a whole hour's worth of sleep! Still, I got to try out my French on the crêpe man. *We had plenty of time for that.*

On Monday morning we all went our separate ways. Caroline and I went to the Arc de Triomphe and we had our photo taken with my snazzy camera (*have I mentioned the camera enough?*). Who did we bump into? None other than Trent and Beccy! *Fancy seeing you here!* The guys kindly offered to give me a little assistance in writing the last few postcards, so we found a café out of the way of the tourist traps and settled down to do some work with coffee and croissants ordered for the umpteenth time as fuel.

Trent left us to go and visit a friend, while Caroline, Beccy and I walked all of the way from the Arc de Triomphe to the *Tour Eiffel*, otherwise known as the Eiffel Tower (just saying). Many people had told us that we should book tickets in advance to guarantee getting up there. Great advice. With a not-so-set itinerary we figured we'd gamble it. We lost. As we got closer we realised that the queues went on for miles. Not ideal at all and the girls wandered on as I scuttled about wondering where I could leave a postcard. *I had to leave a postcard. It's the Eiffel Tower!*

I was struggling. I wasn't sure what to do. I was angry with myself that I hadn't thought this through well enough. I started to give up and headed back to meet the others. As I strolled past, I noticed three girls who were standing in the crowds under the tower and I couldn't help but stop in my tracks. OK, so handing a postcard directly to someone wasn't what the original plan was really about but it was worth a try, right? Of course, they might think I was crazy — I was a girl on her own hanging out at the Eiffel Tower with a postcard in her hand — but I suppose I was crazy, in a way. They looked very friendly, though, so I gave it a go.

As I dashed away, I looked back to see the girls gathered around reading the message. This was the only point in the trip when I really choked up. These strangers now knew why I was in Paris and what it meant to me. I was crying out of joy. I could be sure, this time at least, that someone was reading my message. Strangers were reading about my mum. I felt like a part of my mission was accomplished right there and then.

I found Caroline and Beccy and told them about what had just happened and I cried for the first time in a very long time. I explained how I had a good feeling about this one — about how the connection I made as I handed it to them in person gave me some hope of hearing back. But nothing was guaranteed. I was leaving it to hope — the hope that someone would take a chance on me.

I headed off to meet up with some of the others before they left Paris, while Beccy and Caroline decided to go off on their postcard mission to a bookshop. I would have loved to go too, but there just wasn't time to do everything.

First they went to the Shakespeare and Company bookshop. They said that they played around like kids in there for a good long while 'because it's an Aladdin's cave of book delights', or so Caroline told me. They left a postcard on the piano upstairs in the corner, where a customer was playing. When he wasn't looking, Beccy slipped a postcard behind the sheet music on the piano. He must have found it because he then went to find her and asked her if she was me. She told him she was one of my little helpers. He loved what we were doing and said how it had made his day.

They left one in a book that was a bestseller that December called *Billy Lynn's*

Long Halftime Walk by Ben Fountain, and one in a book that reminded Caroline of a conversation we'd had recently about over-hearing funny snippets of conversation — *Overheard* by Jonathan Taylor. Another was left in the book *Enduring Love* by Ian McEwan, because it seemed appropriate. Beccy said she felt like she could fall in love in the Shakespeare and Company bookshop. She felt an amazing sense of 'what's been before' — all the history and stories waiting to be discovered.

During all of this, Beccy had been nipping about squirrelling postcards into little corners and the girls said that they could tell a few people were wondering what they were up to. They went around the corner to The Abbey Bookshop, which had crazy piles of books everywhere. They left one postcard on a rack of books as you entered the shop — very easy to spot — and one right at the back. Caroline hid one in between two psychology books about coping. It only had the *PLEASE READ/LIS S'IL VOUS PLAIT* line sticking out — I really wish she'd taken pictures but apparently the shop assistant was looking at her suspiciously and there was a guy behind the desk who looked pretty formidable.

Meanwhile, I went off to meet Katie, Kerry and Amy and enjoyed my final lunch in Paris with them. I went for a classic *croque monsieur* to round off the trip nicely. I decided to put a postcard on the table next to me as I left. There were two men on another table nearby who saw what I had done and Katie, in a fluster about what had happened, found herself stuck behind the table with the men staring at her. The rest of us snuck out, being the good friends that we are!

Amy had to scoot off to catch her train — the numbers were dwindling rapidly. Katie, Kerry and I stopped off in a macaroon shop and then it was back to the apartment to tidy up, pack and leave our adventure in Paris behind. I said goodbye to Antoinette and reluctantly handed back her keys. Of course, it would be silly not to hide a postcard in the apartment. I put one on the table, among some papers and another in the book where guests can write. *I wonder who else will be staying in this apartment. Will they find it?*

We left the last few remaining postcards at the Gare du Nord, placing them on a few tables in the café in the main station, and then we boarded the Eurostar, destination King's Cross St Pancras.

As the train set off, we chatted away about the last four days — about the whole adventure, the people, the comedy moments and, of course, the postcards. I sat in my seat

151

and began to feel sad, the post-holiday blues were upon me. But there is nothing like your best friend to pull you out of them. 'What are you doing?' I asked Caroline, as I saw what looked like her writing lines in her notebook. 'Oh,' she replied, as if it was the most normal thing in the world to do, 'I was just trying to write with my left hand — I'd quite like to be ambidextrous.' 'What are you trying to write?' 'Practice makes perfect.'

And with that, I was laughing again.

8

Paris Postcard Found!

When we returned from Paris, we were all back to work by the next day — the weekend had gone in a flash. *I wish I was still there.* However quickly it had whizzed by, that trip was going in personal record books as the most incredible weekend away that I had ever been on. I browsed through the photos and I felt so lucky that my housemates had been there to share the adventure as we could reminisce over our dinners together in our King's Cross home.

As I settled back in to my normal life, I kept trying, so desperately hard, to put any postcard thoughts to the back of my head. It was bitterly cold in Paris, some of the postcards had been left outside — they would be long gone. And the rest — would they ever be found? I had created this project with such high hopes of it giving me a new focus. But what if no one got in touch, could this go the opposite way? Would I end up feeling like a failure? I had tried to do such a special thing

153

for my mum and now I might fall flat on my face. I hadn't even thought about the fact that this project could actually break me. *Oh no, what have I done?* And, to top it all off, the 'first' Christmas was looming over me. I was not feeling festive in any single way. *Please take that tinsel out of my face immediately. I'm not in the mood.*

Three nights after we had returned from The City of Love, I hit the shops on Oxford Street after work, searching for presents for my family and friends before heading to a show with Beccy. She had seen that there was a pantomime on in Clapham, suitable for both adults and children. *Admittedly, I often feel like both of those.* It sounded completely random but neither of us had plans that evening — we thought it could be fun. Whatever happened, I felt it was important to keep busy — continue the buzz that we were feeling from the incredible weekend in Paris.

Off we went with a spring in our step and feeling ready for a good laugh. That was until we realised the story was Cinderella. Hmmm — we were bound to hear a lot of 'your mum is dead' chat. Luckily, it soon became absurd, rather than sad, as they broke into song about it. *Are you kidding me? Should I sing along?* I had been dreading the 'first' Christmas and now I was being subjected to this! *It could only happen to me*. Still, Beccy went down for a dance in the interlude and I felt like a stronger person than I had been a few months ago. This time I was able to laugh. *Finally!*

It was on the overground train back home that evening when I realised Christmas was definitely coming early for me. *I've been good — honest!* My phone vibrated in my hand — I had a new email. The subject read, 'Paris Postcard Found!' This was it! *What a present!* Beccy and I screamed on the train and hugged excitedly as passers-by looked on bemused. *If only they knew.* All I really needed to make the whole thing feel a success was to have one response — just one! And now I had it!

Hello!
My friends (Nashely Ruiz and Rebecca Retana) and I (Arielle Tan) came across one of your postcards in Paris! We found it sitting on top of a pile of books in the music/film section of The Abbey Bookshop in the 5eme. I'm attaching a picture.

Is it possible for us to get the link to your blog? We'd love to check it out!
Thanks,
Arielle

Oh my goodness. *What?* I sent a text to the Paris Crew. We had done it — it was such a good feeling. *I'm buzzing!* This was what I had been waiting for, nervously checking my phone, hoping and wishing that something would come through. But I had no idea where these people were from or what they were doing there.

> ARIELLE!! And Nashely and Rebecca!
> Thank you so, so, so much for your email.
> You really have made me extremely happy!
> It would be amazing if you could send a
> photo of you three and perhaps a little bit
> about yourselves and what you were doing
> together in Paris and in the bookshop.
>   Hope you are having a lovely week.
>   Rachael xxxx

Who are you?! The unknown was part of the thrill. Were they Parisiennes on a trip to their local bookshop? When I heard back from them with details about their backgrounds, I was astonished to find that they were not from Paris at all but from much further afield.

> Arielle:
> I was born in Oakland, CA, grew up in Port-
> land, Oregon, and I returned to the Bay Area

for school. I just graduated from the University of San Francisco in May 2013 and I currently work as a barista in the city. In my spare time, I wander the streets in search of good food and good books.

During my senior year at USF, I studied abroad at the American University in Paris, which is where I met Rebecca and Nashely. The Abbey Bookshop in the 5eme was one of our favorite places to hang out after class, and it was on one of those trips when we saw your postcard sitting on a stack of books!

Nashely:

As Hemingway once wrote 'There are only two places in the world where we can live happy: at home and in Paris.' And so that is exactly where I found myself; in the middle of the Latin Quarter in The Abbey Bookshop when I found your postcard amongst the endless stacks of books. Which, knowing my love for books and the Parisian lifestyle, is no surprise.

I am a recent Graduate from the University of San Francisco, with a major in International Business. I consider myself to be a Philanthropic Entrepreneur. I started my own business, People; a definite hobby of mine. People sells hand-made gifts and all

profit goes to help kids achieve an education. My passion for helping others has
brought me to Westward Leaning, were I
work as an Operations Associate. Westward
Leaning makes sunglasses that celebrate
human achievement by incorporating unique
materials. These two companies occupy
most of my time but I consider myself fortu-
nate to enjoy helping others and of course
taking a trip with friends whenever I get the
chance!

Rebecca:
   I was born in San Antonio, Texas, and
have lived here all my life. And, yes, it is
pretty conservative but the people are really
nice and we really do say y'all a lot
— hahaha. This is my third year of college
and I go to a private Catholic school called
the University of the Incarnate Word
(mouthful, I know). I am majoring in international affairs and minoring in history. I
have a huge family (I'm the youngest of
six). There are two brothers and three sisters, of which the oldest sibling, my brother
Cezar, is like 40 years old — yeah crazy.
Both of my parents are from Mexico and
moved here to work around the late 1960s
early 70s. I don't have a job as of now but I
hope to get an internship in Washington

D.C. in the summer or next fall and build myself up from that.

I was in Paris last fall through a study abroad program at my school (studying abroad is pretty much required for my major). I chose Paris because I wanted to be challenged and I didn't know anyone there, as I was pretty much the only student going to Paris from my college. In a way Paris was for me a sort of new place that would test me on my ability to adapt and be independent, to see if I could handle it. Fortunately I did because of the two amazing friends I made, Nashely and Arielle. The three of us went on another run to The Abbey Bookshop, which became pretty much our favorite place in Paris, or at least I think. Nashely and I were looking at the stacks of books on a bookshelf against the wall, and Arielle went off to who knows where and came back with one of the postcards you sent out. She read it out loud and I couldn't help but wonder how she came across such an awesome thing like that — I mean, this only happens in movies, right? Anyway, we were all pretty touched by what you said and we urged Arielle to go ahead and contact you, since this type of thing does not happen often. It's safe to say that we all thought it was great and were pretty excited to come upon a project that was meaningful and adventurous. It was also a moment that we shared together on our big trip in Paris, and I thank you for that.

I was blown away. *Someone pinch me. Harder than that.* My handwritten note (with just one hundred words) had been picked up by a group of girls who lived on the other side of the world! 60 Postcards had gone global! *This is insane — completely insane.* Even when I had first hatched up my postcard plan, it had totally slipped my mind that the finders could come from around the world. *How did I not think about that?* As soon as I started to receive their news, I wanted to grab my phone straight away. And guess who I wanted to call the minute that I got that first response? Mum, of course. *She would love this.*

I felt giddy — I could not believe that my plan had worked. I called my family to tell them that some girls had found one of my postcards and they were all so pleased for me. I had put my heart and soul into that tribute and everyone must have been a little worried for me that I might not get one single email. But I had and now I could relax. If that was the only message I received of all the sixty postcards I had left then I still considered it a success. I promised myself that I would stop checking my phone constantly. *Give it a rest.*

★ ★ ★

Just two days later I wandered through Winter Wonderland in Hyde Park. The normally peaceful park had been transformed into a Christmas fair full of rides, stalls and a band stand with an ice rink surrounding it. I would say that it is up there with the Southbank for Christmas joy. I was meeting Clare for her birthday — we had booked ourselves in to do some ice skating and planned to celebrate afterwards with mulled wine and beers in the Bavarian-style bar. Now it felt like Christmas! *It really doesn't feel 'tis the season to be jolly' until you are slipping around on the ice like Bambi with red-stained teeth!*

When I found Clare, I told her all about the message I had received from Arielle and her friends. She was so excited for me but the magic did not end there — just three hours before our Winter Wonderland date, I had found another email waiting in my inbox. It was early Christmas present number two! *Seriously — I must have been very good this year!*

Rachael,
Here is the photo we took of your postcard at the top of the Eiffel Tower! :) My friends Pam, Ellie and I were all moved by the message on the back of your postcard, and we feel very touched that you asked us to take part in the project. It is such a wonderful idea, and we wish you the best of luck with the other 59 postcards :)

Hope it all went well and that you had a fantastic time in Paris!

Take care,

Beccy

I was lucky to have found this email. It had been lying in my spam folder. Of course — I would be receiving emails that were not on my contacts list and could easily fall into that category. But, yet again, this had not crossed my mind. *Check your spam more often now, you fool.* I sent off a message to Beccy, just as I had done to Arielle, asking her to tell me a little bit more about her:

BECCY!
I have just found your amazing email sitting in my spam folder — so glad I found it:)

Thank you so much for taking it up there, the photo and for sending this email. I really appreciate it. And out of all of the postcards

I left around, I was genuinely hoping to hear back from you guys. I just thought you were so lovely, especially as I was simply a random girl handing you a postcard!

I would absolutely love it if you could send me a photo of the three of you and perhaps a little bit about each of you and what you were doing in Paris?

Hope you are having a good week. I am off to do some last-minute Christmas shopping.

Merry Christmas to you lovely ladies,
Rachael xxx

I knew I had a good feeling about that moment when I passed them the postcard. I could tell that they were younger than me, but they had very much reminded me of my friends and I exploring the city. They had been smiling, laughing and chatting away. I was so lucky that they had been there. *I definitely picked the right people to pass a postcard to — fate.* The more I think about these responses, the more I realise how much I love them. I couldn't believe that my simple idea was providing such amazing stories!

I have attached a photo we took outside the Louvre, the day after we climbed the Eiffel

Tower! And no, your eyes are not deceiving you, Ellie is in fact holding a ukulele! The three of us decided to 'form a band' at uni last year (Three Octaves Down is what we call ourselves), and we even made ourselves band t-shirts, much to the delight/disgust of our other housemates! Ha ha! Excellent pro-crastination technique if nothing else :P

We were in Paris for just under a week, after having spent the past five months apart. Ellie and I both study Modern Languages and a compulsory part of our degree is a Year Abroad. So Ellie has been in Spain since the end of August, and I have just recently moved to Germany after having spent four months in France. We met at the University of Durham; Pam has since gradu-ated and is now studying in London, and Ellie and myself will be returning to Durham in October!

University friends — brilliant! My university years were some of the best of my life and I hoped now that finding this postcard would not only be a wonderful memory for me to keep, but for those girls, too.

I had been so disappointed not to make it to the top of the Eiffel Tower that day, but this was so much better. The message in my mum's memory had made it to the top

— overlooking the whole city where the rest were scattered.

After my trip to Winter Wonderland, and with two postcard finder emails under my 60 Postcards belt, I couldn't wait to tell more people about it. A few days later we hosted a house party (*festive attire was strongly encouraged*) and, as I moved around the kitchen and lounge that evening, I talked about the postcards a lot. I found myself starting almost every single conversation with, 'You will not believe what happened!' Finally, after months of feeling like all my conversations were either about Mum, or were using all of my energy to avoid talking about Mum, now I had good news to deliver. *I love this. Yep — I could definitely get used to it!*

After feeling so anxious about the Christmas holidays — going home without the smell of Mum's chutney, settling down to watch a film with her or watching her open her presents — these emails from strangers had given me a new lease of life. For the first time since my mum's death ten months ago, I was finally travelling home with a smile on my face. *I never thought that it would be possible.*

I travelled back to Dorset by train — I rarely went by coach now unless I absolutely had to, after all of those journeys back and forth in the traumatic two weeks and two days of Mum's deterioration, particularly that last agonising trip the night before she died. I wasn't going back to my family home, though — and I was going to have to start getting used to the idea. *I have to try to get used to it.* My dad had moved house in July, just five months after Mum passed. So many people asked me at the time how I felt about it. But, honestly, although I knew that it would be a very strange transition, it was ultimately the best thing for Dad. *That is the most important thing.* He needed a fresh start in a new environment — not to live in the place where we had spent so many happy years and then so many short days watching her leave us. Still, it meant that this Christmas was going to be very different all round. *It will never be the same again anyway.*

My dad's new house was in Wimborne, just minutes away from the centre of town. *The pubs are closer now — this could be dangerous.* It wouldn't have been right if I hadn't had to power around the shops in Poole getting some last-minute bits and pieces just two days before Christmas. I had told all of the family excitedly about my 60 Postcards news. Hannah, in particular, was so engrossed in my story and kept saying that she felt like it sounded like a story and not real life — she couldn't believe it was actually happening to me. *Nor can I!* But, much to my surprise and delight, while I was out shopping that day, I received the first of two new emails from finders. I was going to have even more news to deliver when I got home!

Dearest Rachael,
    I found one of your postcards in Terminus Nord more than a week ago. On the Ground. First I was attracted by the picture, then I was reading your words and I appreciate your symbolic gesture.
    I wish you a merry Xmas and a fantastic end of the year.
    Kind regards,
    J.P.

On the ground? *Brilliant!* When I had left the Gare du Nord I most definitely hadn't thrown one on the floor (*at least I don't think so!*). In which case, it must have fallen or had perhaps been thrown to the ground by someone who hadn't understood what it said (*charming*). I am just grateful that it didn't end up in the bin! I sent off an email to J.P. to find out more . . .

Later that day, while back at home with my family, still over the moon about the email, I received another message. This really was turning out to be a good Christmas, after all!

Hi Rachael,
My name is Ivan and I am Luxembourgish; I've just returned from Paris last night from a three-day visit.

First of all: THANK YOU very much for doing it. I found your postcard in The Abbey Bookshop, hidden between a bunch of psychology-related volumes. These are the kind of things that turns life even more interesting from time to time. I shot a picture of it instantly, didn't want to miss that moment, or just tried to bring it to an everlasting state. Don't believe too much on that concept, but I felt I had to do it anyway.

Now, my debt to you is to explain what I was doing there at that moment. Well, as many other tourists I love that city, and got trapped in that tiny library looking for something, guessing what could be of any interest to somebody who lives in southeastern Spain. What shocked me as time was going by was that I couldn't find what I was looking for; my theme-targets were mainly astrophysics and/or Chinese calligraphy, but nothing seemed to appear. Then I saw the postcard sticking a couple of inches out of a shelf. Just a coup de glance among a million.

Please keep me informed of your project, and don't hesitate to ask for any other details.

Keep on that way, she'll appreciate it forever.

Yours,

Ivan

His last comment warmed my heart. 'Keep on that way, she'll appreciate it forever.' That was such a kind thing to say from one stranger to another. I was so pleased that he had not only found my card and responded but was so charming about the idea. Messages like this make it all worth it. It's part of the magic. It showed me that anyone in the world can appreciate how difficult it is to lose someone. I took comfort in his words and prepared my response back:

Hi Ivan,

A Merry Christmas to you.

Thank you so much for responding to my postcard message. I really, really appreciate it. I left 60 postcards around Paris in all sorts of places — book shops, on the Métro, in postcard racks, in cafés, telephone boxes, photo booths . . . you name it, we left it. I even handed a postcard to some girls at the bottom of the Eiffel Tower and they sent me an email with a picture of it at the top!

I am actually in Dorset (south coast of England) at the moment where I am from originally — seeing my family for a week. I am working on the blog at the moment and once I have a few more responses I will publish. It will be for family and friends but hopefully people will forward it on to other people. It would be great if you could send a photo of yourself for the blog — but only if you don't mind, of course.

I hope you are having a nice Christmas break.

All the best and I hope to hear from you again sometime,

Rachael x

I had been a little confused by the mentions of Luxembourg and Spain and I couldn't wait to hear more about Ivan and his story.

I was born in San Sebastian, northern Spain, right on the border with France. While growing up my main hobbies were body-boarding and music. At the age of 17 I had an accident that partially paralyzed my legs, but with the priceless help of my parents and friends I could continue living what is called a 'normal' life. I moved then to a southern region and had video and television studies, which enabled me to work in that field for a while.

In 1999 I moved to Luxembourg, just to try and see how life was in central Europe . . . I fell in love with the country till the point I changed my nationality! Many people ask me 'why', and I used to think that 'identity' doesn't necessarily mean 'nationality'. One belongs to a place only when being able to feel it . . . and only one knows when that happens. In other words, countries they don't move from their position, but people do.

I'm 36, and I work as a video editor/director. The reason I was in Paris those days was my health; I had some rough news on those times and I thought I was going to be operated on and lose some of my movement autonomy for a while, so I decided to do that trip to offer myself something good before the 'crisis', let's say. They didn't operate me because nobody knows how to do it in this country, and I've been seeing doctors during these months in search of somebody who could manage with the problem (a bone infection: ostheomyelitis). Finally, and, oh, of course, as another casualty, it seems that somebody from a hospital in Paris could do it — microsurgery — and I'm just waiting for them to answer and get ready for the job.

I don't like to mention my health mess, it makes me being ashamed when people start the 'oh poor you' drama. It is not necessary at all, and I'm pretty sure you've experienced something similar when your mum was gone. So I guess you won't do it neither.

It is now a part of me, I live with it and I must admit it too. I was born in the Basque Country and Spanish is my mother tongue; sorry for my not-enough-oiled English.

Once again, I will never be thankful enough telling you how I appreciate your project and the fact of crossing it in my existence.

It was that comment about 'oh poor you' that I honed in on immediately. I could completely relate to that, of course. So as I was in Paris on my personal journey, Ivan had been on one of his own. He had also been using that break to enjoy his time, while also having such a huge thing to deal with in his life. The most beautiful thing about these emails from Ivan was that in both he thanks me. *I don't deserve that.* He is so grateful to be part of this experience and I feel honoured that this inspiring man has become part of it, too.

I had expected it to be a tough and bleak Christmas, and it was difficult maintaining business as usual. My cousin Nicola and her two daughters, Amber and Lucy, came down and there was a lot of film watching, overeating and a few games of Articulate, too. It was sad, though, to be doing everything as we always did — it almost exaggerated the absence of Mum. *I wish she was here.* I kept trying to pluck up the courage to watch the Take That DVD but I couldn't bring myself to do it. *I'm still not ready.* But my birthday tribute for mum was turning Christmas around for me, too. It was leaving a legacy more far-reaching than I could have predicted and I was dying to get back to London to tell all of my friends what had happened over the holidays.

I travelled back up to London on 30th December for a special event. The 'Wellham Games' was to be hosted by Paris Crew member Katie and her family in their house in Twickenham. Living with Katie I had heard several stories of this annual occurrence and I was ordered to attend. Now the Wellham Games is similar to the Olympics, except that instead of athletics, rowing and gymnastics — there are events such as 'lemon bowling', 'twiddle the bottle' and 'orange jousting', all adjudicated by Katie's dad, who takes his role as Games Master very seriously. Perhaps not quite as physically challenging as the Olympics but, trust me, the competition was just as fierce — there were even trophies to be won. *I want one!* I had not spent much time in other family homes recently. But I really did love being there and embraced the fun and laughter as I thought to myself that I must get my dad along for this event someday. *He would love it!*

After fun at Katie's parents' place, the next day we were back in King's Cross and ready to see in the New Year. We had some friends over for drinks and nibbles and headed down to Camino, the local Spanish bar, for the countdown to midnight. I only managed to get to the bar as the clock struck midnight. (I had lost track of time — strange that), so while everyone around me hugged and wished each other a Happy New Year, I was wandering aimlessly trying to find everyone. *Typical me. Happy New Year to myself!*

The next few days after New Year were very quiet and uneventful, as I nursed a serious hangover as per usual. But on the following Saturday I met Paris Crew member Clare at a hotel in Kensington as we decided to treat ourselves to afternoon tea. *La dee da!* We couldn't help but laugh at ourselves, as we looked so out of place. We are the kind of girls who are far more likely to be found having a pub lunch. I took a sip of my bubbles and was about to take a bite of my cucumber sandwich when my phone beeped. *Another one!*

Hi,
I was on rue Lepic (75018) at the Café des Deux Moulins (Amélie Poulain movie) where I'm having a coffee almost every day
. . . when I saw a girl who put a postcard on the table next to mine . . . I read it and I've been touched . . . So here is my story about it.
     Happy birthday to your mother . . . and best for 2013.
     I'm Alexandre from Paris

Yes, Yes, Yes!!! This was one message that I was desperately hoping to get! It was the very first postcard that I had left. I had watched *Amélie* on my return to London (just as I had promised myself) and I couldn't believe I hadn't thought of the film before I went to Paris. *She is my hero!* I loved the fact that the café was obviously his local haunt — I was very jealous of that. *Why can't I live right*

175

next to the Amélie café? I sent a response
back to my new finder.

> Hello Alexandre!
> It is Rachael, the girl who left a postcard on
> the table next to you at Café des Deux
> Moulins in December!
> I am starting a blog to capture the
> responses that I received.
> I would love to hear from you and hear
> more about you. I hope to visit Paris in the
> future and it would be great to meet for a
> coffee!
> I look forward to hearing from you,
> Rachael — Postcard Girl! X

Clare, or 'fun Clare', was the perfect girl to
have around to chat with about this fantastic
news. Not only had she been there in Paris
where the mission had started, but this was
now the second time that I had been with her
on the same day that I had received an email!

Alexandre, without even realising it, had
chosen the perfect day to hit 'send' on his
mail — Clare and I were off to the Royal
Albert Hall that evening to see my mum's
favourite act, the Cirque du Soleil. I had only
ever been with the whole family a couple of
times, years ago — once at the Royal Albert
Hall and once at Battersea Power Station

— but it had a huge impact on our lives as Mum had all of the DVDs, which we watched on repeat at home. She even had a behind-the-scenes one. *How do they do that?!* Mum loved the colours, the costumes, the music and the choreography — she adored it all. I was feeling a little apprehensive about going to see it with Clare, knowing that it could prove to be a trigger that set off the dark feelings once more. I was trying to focus on the fact that I had made it through Christmas and, not only that, had received some postcard responses during the break. But now I really had no reason to worry. Another tribute message had been found. Team that with watching the best circus act in the world and this was set to be a magical night. *Happy days!*

9

The Dancer

Through the power of the postcards I had heard from Arielle and friends, Beccy and friends, JP, Ivan and Alexandre, but what most people did not know was that I had been keeping one message a secret. I had received it just before I came home for Christmas and had decided to keep schtum as I felt like this had the potential to be the most exciting of them all. It was not a very glamorous location to receive the most incredible email of the set — I was snuggled up in bed. I was off work and had enjoyed a lovely lie-in before I woke and checked my phone. I couldn't have jumped out of bed any faster — I was almost bouncing off the ceiling!

Hello Rachael,
My name is Stephanie. I found your post-card at Shakespeare and Co. in Paris last week. I was there visiting a friend who is currently performing in West Side Story at

the Theatre du Chatelet. I just got back home to New York City where I am a ballet dancer. Your postcard was sitting right in front of a Western photo book at the book store and I was interested in what it said. I decided to bring it with me to the Big Apple and put it somewhere here if you don't mind.

I had a fabulous time visiting Paris. It was my second time there, but this time I was with friends so it was much more fun to see all the sights!

You said you were from London on the card. I lived there for six months dancing with Ballet Black, a dance company that is part of the Royal Opera House 2. If you have the opportunity, you should see their season in the spring.

I wish you all the best, and hope to hear back from you!

Stephanie

In this whole experience I knew it was a given that I would learn new things, but the skill of trying not to shout with joy, cry with emotion and refrain from wetting myself with excitement was quite something. (*I did not actually wet myself.*)

I couldn't get my head around the fact that my postcard was now sitting somewhere in

New York City in the U. S. of A.! One of my postcards had travelled there before I had even had a chance to visit myself. *Jealous.* New York was on my list of places that I longed to go. *Oh, it's on the list, all right.* I felt so giddy and suddenly frustrated by the fact that I was not at work and so had no one to share the news with. I picked up my phone and called Paris Crew member Kerry to tell her about Stephanie. She was so excited for me and, soon after our phone call I went on to Facebook to let all the Paris Crew know. As soon as I had done that, I started to write my reply:

Hey Stephanie,
Thanks so much for responding! I was very excited when I received your email. Especially the fact that you are from New York and my postcard has made it across the world. Have you left it somewhere yet? Thank you so much for that!

Also, you are a ballet dancer — that is incredible. I danced when I was young until about 18. It was only ever a hobby for me but, to this day, nothing gives me more of a buzz than dancing! Also my mother loved watching musicals and dance so this made the fact that you found it even more special. I will definitely check out Ballet Black next year!

I am still putting together the blog. It would be great if you could send a photo of yourself or the postcard (if you still have it!) to put on the blog but only if you don't mind.

I hope you are having a lovely Christmas break.

Look forward to hearing from you again,
Rachael x

In finding more out about Stephanie, it transpired that she was born in Utah and raised in Texas and had trained at the Dallas Dance Academy, making her first appearance with Ben Stevenson's Texas Ballet Theater in 2006–07. She had done a stint in London performing with Ballet Black at the Royal Opera House, just as she told me in her message. Ballet Black was created by Cassa Pancho (MBE) as a way to provide dancers of black and Asian descent with inspiring opportunities in classical ballet. I have walked past the Royal Opera House in Covent Garden a thousand times and so I loved that I could picture where she had been. She now dances for a company called the Dance Theatre of Harlem in New York. *I think my jaw just dropped — she is far too cool.*

Wow — a real-life ballet dancer. The reason that I was keeping this one so close to my chest was because it felt just so personal to me. I was more emotional about this message than I had been about any of the others and I felt it had the closest link to my mum.

Mum loved dancing. She used to dance at college and she most definitely handed this passion down to me. It used to be the biggest passion of my life to take part in and is now the biggest passion of mine to watch.

When I was three, my mum signed me up to join Footlight Dance Academy at the Merley Community Centre. From that moment, all the way up until I was eighteen years old I attended dance classes twice a week, if not more. I did ballet, tap and modern and I went to singing and drama lessons, too, not to mention the exams and shows that were thrown in. The shows were my absolute favourite and I felt so grown up getting all dressed up and wearing red lipstick to perform. The feeling of working so hard on a routine, attending all of the rehearsals and then performing on stage was like no other for me. It was everything to me during those years.

The dance school was like a real family. You had all of your friends there and I got on so well with the principal, Nina, who was close friends with my mum at the time. Mum was so involved in taking us there non-stop as my sisters began to join, too, that she ended up becoming secretary of the dance school. But, not only that, she was costume maker, driver and chief cheerleader. She did not miss a single one of our annual shows. And I loved to look out and see her in that audience.

I will never forget the day that I went for an open audition for a part as 'Brigitta' in *The Sound of Music* (a film that had been played continually in our house over the years) at the Bournemouth Pavilion. Both Mum and Nina came along with me — I was up against girls who had agents but my biggest fan and the principal of my dancing school were with me so I was sure to be OK. I made it to the final five — it was crunch time. Alas, the three places available were not for me — I had done my best, just as Mum had told me to. But as I realised that my best was not good enough, my poor mother endured a whole weekend of me wailing into my pillow feeling like an utter failure. A life of showbiz was clearly not for me since I reacted so badly to one rejection. *I could almost hear Mum's sigh of relief!*

Still, I carried on doing what I loved in my second home of the dance school. It wasn't long before Mum's passion began to shine through once more as she started doing adult tap there. Later we were even in the same dance class together. That was not long before I played netball with her at club level, as well — we were enjoying it all together as mother and daughter.

When I went to university, I helped to run the dance society for two years and, on my return to Dorset, I went to work for Nina and had my own commercial classes for the next two years (it was like street dance but, technically, I was making it up). I would use the lounge to make up my choreography (which I loved to do) and Mum would have to make her way around me. Those classes were great as I had the young teenagers in every week. We would start the class going around the group to ask if anyone had any boy issues and I would give my wise(ish) advice and, more often than not, tell them to dump the boys if they were behaving like idiots and move on. But after I stopped those classes, unfortunately, the fun also stopped for me dance-wise. Dancing seemed to fizzle out of my life and I just enjoyed going to *see* shows. *Maybe I should get on with it and start going to some classes again — something else for the 'to-do' list.*

All of these memories came flooding back to me thanks to Stephanie's email. My new connection with a ballet dancer in New York had made me reminisce and appreciate that wonderful connection I had with my mum.

With dance comes music and soon I was remembering how Mum had such a lovely voice — I liked to listen to her hum along to songs. I miss listening to her blasting out *Les Misérables* or a bit of Adele while she makes our tea. My dad played the guitar when we were little but, I must say, he can't hold a tune quite like Mum could. We used to have hours of fun getting Dad to match a note that we would sing to him. *No chance — never going to happen.* We loved him playing the guitar to us, though. Of course, with Dad being, well, Dad, he would often make up funny songs. 'The Wibberly, Wobberly Monster' was our particular favourite — it was a song that made absolutely no sense, really, but still made my sisters and I giggle away. *No danger of Jay Z snapping that one up.*

The power of music never ceases to amaze me. We all have those tunes that get to us; that can really make us think, laugh or cry. Some songs can send you to sleep or make you want to dance all night. I find music so emotive and have noticed that when you lose someone it can take just a few notes of a song to trigger a reaction. 'All You Need is Love' has a totally different meaning now. And 'Fight for this Love' by Geordie Cheryl was going to be my anthem for helping Mum fight — but I didn't get a chance to use it.

Since Mum and I had shared the Take That Christmas moment, their songs had been just too difficult for me to listen to. On top of that, just as Hannah had realised with her *Mamma Mia* moment, I realised that Mum was not crying because of the music. I believe that my mother knew that she was dying. She knew this would be our last chance to watch it together. *The chorus to 'Pray' means so much more now.*

On the day that Mum died, I went up to my room and I put 'Back for Good' on repeat. I wanted to train myself to be able to listen to it. *I know I sound like a schoolgirl.* But it hadn't worked. Only a few months later, I was on my way to the cemetery and I decided to go to the florist to buy a rose. As I walked into the shop, what song came on the radio? Yes — of all the songs in the world. I found it comforting then and I have been able to listen to it ever since. *Watching the DVD is sure to be a different story, though.*

Mum and I watched lots of dance together, from ballets to musicals — anything and everything. My favourite of all was going to see *Billy Elliot* in London and, as it is set in 'Geordieland man', it made her feel at home and I did, too, as Mum still had her accent. With every 'Pet' I heard it made me smile.

She used to love *Strictly Come Dancing*, *Britain's Got Talent* and *Got to Dance*, the reality talent shows. We were midway through a series of *Got to Dance* when Mum died. Mum had watched the audition stage with me and told me that she thought the Irish modern tap dancers Prodijig would win. When they did, I thought to myself, 'Mums are always right!' In the semi-final after Mum had passed, Diversity performed on the show. It reminded me that I had been with Mum and my whole family to watch Diversity's first audition on *Britain's Got Talent* years ago. I wouldn't be surprised to find that I am responsible for almost half of the YouTube hits for that semi-final guest performance. I was so upset that Mum could not see it that I watched it on repeat for days on end. *I've seen it so much now, I could give it a go myself.*

Stephanie's message reminded me of my love and my mum's love for dance — a love that perhaps faded a little when Mum died as I was so sad to see anything without being able to experience it with her, or at least tell her about it. I went to see a show in the summer after she passed called *Some Like it Hip Hop* (at Sadler's Wells sister theatre). Not happy with going once, I ended up going a massive (and completely mad) four times.

OK, I deservedly got a lot of stick for that. But, you know what — it was the first dance performance that I went to see that year that didn't make me sad. Mum and I used to watch so many things together and we got so excited together. The show was amazing — it had been the first thing I had seen that had made me look forward to dancing again.

★   ★   ★

Not long after receiving Stephanie's email, I received a message from my housemate Beccy asking me to keep a date free in my diary for February, but she wouldn't tell me what we were doing. I had become much closer to all of Beccy's family over the past few years and her mum, Sue, was coming down for the evening and they said they had a night out planned for me. It was a surprise and I had absolutely no idea what was going on. *I want to know right now!* Still — I was forced to wait. *OK — maybe the surprise is better!*

In the meantime, the biggest milestone of them all was approaching — the one-year anniversary of my mother's death. We had all spoken as a family and decided that perhaps we shouldn't get together for it and thought we would be better off doing our own things.

It made sense, if we were all in one place we would undoubtedly find ourselves wallowing and miserable. I changed my mind time and time again about what the best thing was for me to do. I took the day off work, for a start, as did Caroline to join me. I knew that I wouldn't be able to stomach staring at a computer screen all day and to be faced with cheery faces when I would be feeling so glum. We spent the day in coffee shops and we ended the evening in a bar near my house, where I invited the Paris Crew and a few others to come and raise a glass to Mum. I really thought that it was a good idea at the time. *Have I just organised a party to celebrate my mum's death? What was I thinking? Where is Dynamo when you need him to make you disappear?* Still, anything was better than sitting at home on my own and it was great to have my closest friends surrounding me for support.

A few days later and Beccy announced that she could finally reveal the grand plan. After Beccy had told her mum about Stephanie's response, Sue got off the phone and did some research on Ballet Black. Sue had managed to get us tickets to see a dress rehearsal of *War Letters*, a Ballet Black performance at the Royal Opera House. Stephanie's recommendation was going to become a reality — I couldn't believe it! *I've always wanted to see something at the Royal Opera House!* I wished the week would pass as quickly as possible so I could be there.

On the evening of the dress rehearsal we arrived in plenty of time and Beccy and I had our photo taken underneath the London and New York clocks, not wanting to miss such a glaringly obvious sign. We made our way to our seats and I was buzzing with excitement.

A dress rehearsal is a fantastic thing to go and see. You get a running commentary throughout from the choreographer and you are let in on the deeper meaning of the story behind the dances, not to mention being walked through the routine, which shows you just how much it takes to get a piece as perfect as possible. The dances that we saw rehearsed were absolutely beautiful — I couldn't help but shed a tear at one of the most moving pieces. I thought about Mum and how much she would have loved to see this and I felt sad that there were so many shows that she was never going to be able to see.

A Question and Answer session followed the performances as members of the company were joined by the founder of Ballet Black, Cassa Pancho, and the choreographer, Christopher Marney. When the evening came to a close, Beccy, Sue and I had a brainwave. If they were still hanging around the stage, I had to try to meet Cassa to tell her the story of how I came to watch the show that evening. Beccy and her mum were the perfect people to have around to encourage me to do this as they pushed me off, shouting, 'Go, go, go!'

I moved forward against the grain of the crowd of people filtering out of the theatre and went down the stairs to sneak as close to the stage as I could when I was stopped in my tracks by a theatre steward. I explained to the man that I was trying to find Cassa Pancho to speak to her, if she was available. *Please say that she is!* They told me that I couldn't go any further and that I would have to wait at the front of house in case she came out that way. *Fine — spoil sport.* It seems luck was on my side, though, because, just as I was about to head back to the main foyer, I noticed that one of the dancer's from the Q&A session was coming through from the front and was heading right in my direction.

I stopped the man and asked if he could spare a couple of minutes. His name was Damien Johnson and he had been performing as part of the company for years. I gave a brief summary of my 60 Postcards story and explained that a ballet dancer had found one of my messages. When he asked who it was and I told him about Stephanie, I was shocked and ecstatic to hear that Damien knew her. *It is a very small world!* They had danced with Ballet Black at the same time and, not only that, but it turns out they are both from the same place originally! This really was turning out to be a night to remember. Damien promised me that he would pass on the message to Cassa and the team, and I went off on my merry way feeling more than happy with my latest mission's success. *60 Postcards had come back to London via New York!*

So, let me just repeat it to myself, because it baffles me every single time — I met a dancer in the Royal Opera House who knows the ballet dancer living in NYC, who happened to pick up my handwritten postcard in a bookshop in Paris. I never, ever expected anything like this to happen.

We left the auditorium in a frenzy of excitement but the fun wasn't about to stop just yet. We bumped into the choreographer, Christopher Marney, as he was leaving the theatre. *Poor him!* I relayed my postcard story once again as he listened intently. He is not only a talented and well-respected choreographer but he is also a dancer who has performed with several companies and has been involved in some of Matthew Bourne's works, too. I asked for a quick photo and then we made a dash for the door before anyone had a chance to put a restraining order on me for hassling the Ballet Black crew! *It is only a matter of time before I get arrested for my postcard antics, surely?*

Oh, what a night! How am I ever going to top this one? *You never know . . .*

10

Sharing the Magic

My evening watching Ballet Black and meeting Damien Johnson and Chris Marney had been the highlight of my month. I had a lovely email exchange with Stephanie before and after seeing the show.

Hi Stephanie,
I just wanted to let you know that after I told my friend all about your email, she then called her mum to tell her the story. Her mum then went ahead and booked tickets to see the dress rehearsal for Ballet Black's performance. I am going tonight! Thank you very much for recommending.
I will let you know what I think.
Rachael x

Rachael,
Wow! I hope you enjoyed it. I want to drop your postcard off soon. I'll send you a picture of it and myself!
Stephanie

Hey,
It was incredible! I loved it. Especially the commentary through the rehearsal and seeing them tweak the dances. I bumped into a dancer called Damien Johnson and the choreographer Christopher Marney and told them why I was there.
It was magical :)
Have a lovely day.
Speak soon x

In Stephanie's words, 'Wow.' My postcard was going to be left somewhere in New York and I liked the fact that, at this point, I had no idea where. My passion for this project was growing with every single email from a finder and 60 Postcards was all I wanted to talk about. Texting, Facebooking and calling my friends to ramble on about it all was becoming a little tiresome for me, let alone them. *What is it with the glazed eyes? This is postcard magic!* It was time to start thinking about the blog. It was time to share my story. *I need to tell everyone what has happened!*

In those months and weeks after I got back from Paris, the magic of the responses that I received should have spurred me on to start the blog straight away. I had even mentioned on my postcard message that I would be documenting it in this way — the finders would be waiting. But my procrastination came about due to the dark and gloomy cloud of misery that was still looming very closely over my head.

I hadn't heard of anything quite like what I was doing and I knew that in speaking out about the postcard fun, I would also have to explain exactly why it had all started — I was wondering if it was safer to keep those thoughts to myself and lock them away in my head. I was likely to have to delve into the ins and outs of my grieving process and it was a huge thing for me to do. I worried that people may feel it was an over-share or that it may make some readers feel uncomfortable. My friends reassured me that if there were any people who felt that way, they could simply choose not to read it. Even so, I knew that it was going to be a huge thing for me to talk about — it may make me too vulnerable. I have never been a mysterious character, always wearing my heart on my sleeve, but was this one step too far?

With the one-year anniversary of my mother's death now behind me (I felt like I had blinked and that year had gone far too quickly) and with my family rooting for me and supporting the idea, I decided that it was time to get to work. And, besides, by now I had spoken to so many friends and strangers face to face about the project with such positive and excited reactions, that I was almost bursting at the seams to tell so many more. I was ready to ditch the 'fear' and get the blog started up!

My housemate Beccy had spotted the perfect one-hour blogging course for me at the Women of the World Festival at the Southbank Centre and I signed up almost immediately. It was in March 2013 and I met Caroline, who was going to do the course with me, outside the front of the Royal Festival Hall and we headed in. Anyone walking into this place would struggle not to be inspired by what was going on all around the building. It is a hive of activity of folks socialising and working, while a group of dancers are often found on the bottom floor running through their latest routine. (*I have to hold myself back from joining in.*)

We walked into the course room to find it filled with around thirty to forty people, and we took our place on one of the round tables at the back, with a smile and a 'hello' to those already sitting down. The feng shui of the room screamed 'interaction' and I began to feel very nervous. We got our notepads and pens out like the good students that we are and Katie Welsh, a pro-blogger and writer, began to introduce the course. She gave a rundown of the agenda and then got straight to the first point, 'What should you blog about?' She explained to us that there was no point in setting up a blog unless the over-arching theme was something that you were intensely passionate about. *Tick*. I felt better already. There is nothing I could be more passionate about than my wonderful mother and telling the world about her. It was at this point that I was one hundred per cent certain that I was doing the right thing.

We were encouraged to talk to the people around us about our ideas — there was everything from science blogs and school blogs to blogs on feminism and politics. It was my turn and I couldn't keep the smile from my face when those listening gave me the most wonderful feedback. I began to wish the time away so that I could get started.

The minute I got home, I set up my WordPress account and chose a simple theme, a colour scheme and I had a play around with how it all worked. It was fun already and I hadn't even started the writing part. I wanted the introduction to be short and sweet, with a brief description of what was yet to come. I wanted to make a promise to the reader. It was so important for me to explain that this was not going to be a blog of misery. It would be honest, yes — but not depressing. That would be no fun for anyone. I decided that, given the nature of my story, photos were vital — as they would help tell the tale along the way. To make them unique I would write notes in handwriting on them. Everything was going to plan and now I just needed to pluck up the courage to publish the first post. Having got everything in place, I waited one more night before starting. The next day was 10th March 2013 — Mother's Day. It would make the perfect gift:

Starting a blog is scary. Really scary. I've been procrastinating for too long now though. It's time to ditch 'the fear' and get going. So here I am. Hi.

People always say that if you are going to blog, make sure it is something that you are passionate about. Tick. There is nothing I could be more passionate about than my wonderful mother and telling the world about her. When she died I really wasn't sure how I'd be in a year but I am still standing. Admittedly, I am reduced to a crawl when I've been on the vino blanc, but you get my drift. I'm mainly standing.

Rather than just rambling on and on, I am setting myself creative challenges to spread the word about Mum. I will write about these on here whilst telling you a few stories of past and present along the way. This is not going to be a morbid read for you, I promise you that. More smiles, less tears. It's about battling through the pain of losing someone and doing something special. Something beautiful. My mum would have loved this, which is exactly why I am doing it.

I've got big ideas, small ideas and even ideas involving the readers of this blog. (If I get any. Awkward.) I want this to be a good read for anyone that stumbles across it (or is forced to read it by me standing over their computer — watch out). So many people seem to be afraid of talking about the loss of a loved one. I don't think it should be such a taboo subject and I want to try something new. If this inspires anyone then that's a bonus.

I am going to be posting regularly, assuming I don't forget my password. 'What a stupid thing to do?' I hear you say. Well, you are listening to a girl who lost two bank cards within a month. Anything is possible. Sometimes I even surprise myself.

Come back again to find out what happened when I left a message on 60 postcards around Paris.

There is a reason I posted this today. Happy Mother's Day to my inspiration.

Ciao for now.
Rachael

I tried not to pay too much attention to the blog statistics but I soon found that it was as addictive as popping bubble wrap or devouring rich tea biscuits. *You just can't stop!* The fact that you can see where people are when they are viewing your blog is also fascinating — a colourful map shows where in the world it has been read.

When I first started the blog I said to Caroline how amazing it would be if I could get to one thousand views and that I would think about a way to celebrate when that happened in a year's time, or so, whenever I might reach that milestone. I nearly fell off my chair when I hit the one thousand mark after two days. *This is unbelievable!*

I had an absolutely amazing response from family and friends who were beginning to hear about the blog through the power of Facebook, Twitter and through word of mouth. The family comments from up North and around the world were wonderful. I was the most nervous about their responses because I was talking about someone that was in their life, too, and who they loved dearly. Would it be too much for them to read? The feeling was unanimous, though — they fully approved of my plan. And I was so glad — I wanted this to be a gift for us all.

'Hope you know I am an avid reader and when I first read why you were writing I had a little tear in my eye but joy in my heart. Keep it up love, Steve xx' [Mum's brother]

'Hello Rach. The Canadian wing of the family is avidly reading your posts, too. Thanks for doing this. It's been over a year, but I still find the emotions are close to the surface when I think of Viv. I guess things stay raw longer when it's your younger sister who has passed away.
    'Recently, after years of talking about it, I've actually started to sort through box after box of photographs and naturally some of my favourites are the ones of the family. Many of these are of our holidays in Devon, Cornwall, Morzine, Stressa and in and around Northumberland, of course. As I worked my way through them I came across photos of our cottage near Wells and was of course reminded of the 'killer-cow' incident. It's now part of family folklore, but for those who don't know, Viv managed to convince five adults and at least six children that our only hope of surviving a walk across a meadow was to climb a fence and wade

across a stream to escape a cow that was getting uncomfortably close. Now it turned out this cow was the most friendly creature ever to walk the planet, but to Viv it was a threat to her family and she had to act. With hindsight we may have overreacted a bit, but Viv was driven to protect her brood and none of us were going to stop her.

'Looking forward to more posts R. Thinking about Viv and the Chadwicks often.' [Graham — Mum's brother]

This was so lovely to hear. I was going back home for Dad's birthday and I was excited to show him what I'd done so far. I was still concerned about whether he was really OK with me sharing my story, a part of our family's history, in this way.

On my first day back, though, it was time to head to a recording studio (*I'm working on my new album — OK, not so much*). We had bought Sarah some hours in a recording studio for her birthday and she had been waiting for a time when I could go with her. I was so excited to share the experience. (*I was secretly warming my voice up in case there was a chance for a duet.*) It was so heart-warming to listen to her amazing voice and to see her doing what she loved. She had found performing at concerts very difficult since Mum had passed — Mum had never missed a show. We listened back to her CD when we got home and it was perfect. (*She is her own worst critic and she thought she could have done better, but it was perfect.*)

We took Dad to the Tickled Pig, a fancy new restaurant in the little town of Wimborne for his birthday dinner. We gave him his presents, one of which was a new wallet, and we all laughed and despaired as he decided to exchange all of his cards and coins just as the dinner was being served. It was most definitely an improvement on his birthday the year before and it was good for us all to be together — back as a team. I was chuffed to learn that he had signed up to the blog and had even begun telling his friends about it. That was all I could wish for — my family were on board. *On with the writing!*

I was receiving so many messages of support telling me to keep going. It was exactly the reassurance I needed. I started to blog twice a week and people began to follow me by email. The most incredible part of it was that people who had also lost loved ones were getting in touch to say they could relate to it. With that in mind and after chats with my friends, I decided that, if this was going to help people, I wanted to reach out to more readers. On my return to London, I decided to take a leap of faith. I contacted the Editor of *Stylist* magazine, the London weekly women's publication, explaining what my blog was about and asked if they could possibly mention it somewhere. I waited for a couple of days and then received an email from the Deputy Editor of *Emerald Street*, which is the email newsletter linked with *Stylist*. She wrote to me saying that they wanted to mention my blog in one of their emails. Wow! When I asked what their readership was, I was thinking a few thousand. It was, in fact, *ninety* thousand. The email came out as I was on my way to work one morning and when I looked at my blog statistics I couldn't believe the boom on the graph. The domino effect had started. At first I had been talking to myself on a computer screen and then I was talking to lots of familiar faces as friends and family started to read it. Now, after the email from *Emerald Street* had been sent out, I realised that the majority of my readers had become people who had no idea who I was. And I didn't know anything about them. It was complete and utter madness. I had also received messages from a couple of journalists, a literary agent and a book publisher. *This really is crazy.*

In the meantime, the responses to the blog

were coming in every week and were making me so happy. I was hearing from people from all different areas of my life. One of the most emotional to read came from the GP family friend who had helped Mum when she was so ill — someone who my mum spoke of with such kindness:

> 'Hi Rachael, I'm reduced to tears reading this and the battery on my computer is about to run out. I bumped into your dad earlier today who told me about this project! It is wonderful and reminds me of many things of my dad who I lost. Well, I didn't really lose him, in fact I think I found him as I have since remembered lots of little foibles we have shared in the family over the intervening 5½ years! This is truly inspirational and I intend to share with family, friends and patients alike. I look forward to following it. I am a virgin blogger.' [Andy — GP and family friend]

The magic of my postcard story was even bringing people in touch who I hadn't seen for years:

> 'Rach your story continues to leave tears in my eyes and excitement in my heart. But it's not a story it's real — real life excitement

that I'm loving living with you. I'm so smiley about how it's all threading together in small pieces by accident. It's amazing. Outstanding even. I admire your bravery for starting it and I hope it never ends. xxxxx' [Jenna — an old friend from dance school]

This one gets me every single time:

'Hi Rach, It's been a long time since we have communicated, years in fact. Music is very important to me, too, and I think, like you say, in time you will be able to listen to Take That songs and watch the Progress DVD at some point when you're ready, whenever that is! Your mum was a very proud and passionate woman, in her career and family life. I know from a personal point of view how it feels to lose a parent when we are so young! My dad died in April 2010 of a brain tumour, that was diagnosed as malignant and we had six weeks to get our head around everything until he left us. People say it gets easier with time, and you just want to punch them in the face or yell at them, it's been three years this year, and it still feels like yesterday when you relive it. We all have our good days and bad days, and we all deal with it in different ways, too. I can't listen to Luther Vandross

— Dance With My Father — I cry all the
way through it still! Things are different; we
adjust, but never forget. I am sure your
mum will be so proud of what you are
doing, and together with her in your heart,
you will have a little bit of 'Patience', 'Shine'
and you will also 'Rule the World'. Big hugs
to you xxxx' [Clare — an old school friend
who used to live at the end of our road]

Many of Mum's colleagues and good friends
sent me comments. A lot of whom said they
found it hard to talk about Mum in school as
it was too difficult — others found they
talked about her all the time:

'Oh wow that's amazing! Who would have
thought those postcards would have brought
you so many new experiences and friends.
Someone up there is definitely watching
over you! Liz Y x' [Liz — Mum's good
friend who helped me clear her classroom]

'Was just about to write a very thoughtful
comment and then Amy appeared by my
side unable to sleep because she was too
tired. I was tired too and wanted to get on
with replying to you and get on with the
other jobs I needed to do . . . and then I
stopped thinking about myself and took

inspiration from your blog. I always admired your mum, she was an amazing mum to you, she always seemed to have time for your needs and nothing was too much for her girls. I always wanted to be like her and so I put my needs and the computer aside and cuddled up with Amy and rubbed her tummy and realised there is nothing more important than caring for her and showing her that she is more important than any-thing else. I felt better, she fell asleep and our bond strengthened even more. Thank you for reminding me that spending time showing love to one another is more pre-cious than anything else in this life. Miss you, too, Viv, you inspired me in so many ways and you, Rachael, and your amazing family are creating an incredible legacy for your mum to be very proud of. Your words are truly making a difference to so many people's lives.' [Sandy — Mum's work col-league and good friend]

'Took me a while to read this blog . . . but wonderful as ever . . . tears and laughter as always . . . love it! Love you my amazing god daughter! Such a beautiful way to remember her . . . good on the Chaddies! Xxx' [Aunty Tinky]

And the most mind-boggling messages for me, were from people that I have never even met:

'Hi Rachael, I have been reading your story and loving it all — what a fabulous idea to commemorate your mum and how she still inspires you. I wonder at what point a follower of your blog will find a postcard! Imagine how excited they will be! Vohn x' [Blog reader]

'Hi Rachael, I have just discovered your blog via Emerald Street, and have sat through my lunch hour transfixed. I have shared this on Facebook so my friends can discover it, too. This is a beautiful way to remember your mum, and it is nice to read such a lovely story instead of my usual lunchtime news reading, which is so often depressing!' [Blog reader]

'Please come to Stirling, Scotland, and leave postcards here so that I can be part of this great idea. I, too, am looking forward to the next instalment. More please, KC.' [Blog reader]

The messages that were some of the most difficult to read, however, were also the biggest push to keep me going — messages from both friends and strangers who had lost someone, too, or who were in the process of coping with a loved one being ill:

'Hi Rachael, I just wanted to tell you what a lovely idea this is, your mum would have loved it! I lost my mum when I was 25 and she was 60, she was a teacher, too, like Viv and touched so many people's lives. You are so right to keep talking about her and telling lots of stories. Be really proud to be her daughter, that's what I still try to do even after 22 years. Hope things are good with you. Look forward to reading more! Jo xx'
[Family friend from holidays in Cornwall]

'Hi Rachael,
'I started reading your blog after it was featured in Emerald Street, and I think it is such a wonderful way to pay tribute to your Mum.
   'Your recent posts have really hit home, as my mum is battling ovarian cancer, which she was diagnosed with in late 2011. She's been through operations, chemo, radiation, a trial, clots and many meds, but it's now about making her as comfortable as possible, which has meant a stay in the hospice to sort out her meds, in between regular

hospital visits/stays, home visits and many ups and downs along the way, so everything is all very day-by-day.

'You said with your blog that people may think you've dealt with your grief and sadness, but the blog just helps as a focus. I understand what you mean, as I use all sorts of things to focus on to distract me, and even though friends think I'm being 'so brave' and dealing with it really well, I certainly don't feel like I am. It's made harder as she lives in New Zealand and I live in London, so I can't see her regularly. I flew home when she was admitted to the hospice, but am back in London again now, but am planning another trip next month.

'I think this project you have started is such a brave thing to do, when at times you must just feel so sad, especially as you mentioned when you want nothing more than for your mum to share in the excitement of 60 Postcards' success. However, I hope that seeing your mum's story live on through all the lovely letters you've received and the amazing response you've had to your postcards has helped you, as you do something so positive to remember her.

'Your blog has certainly inspired me and I hope it has helped you too.

'All the very best xx' [Blog reader]

And, while all of this was going on in my life, many of my colleagues were also reading online. I loved going into the office after a blog instalment had been published — the girls on my team and I would grab a coffee and gather around the table in between our desks and have a good old mothers' meeting (choice words!) about it all. We giggled as they would ask me what happens next but then suddenly stop — 'No, I want to wait for the next one!' They were encouraging me wholeheartedly and they were often first to hear my blog news before anyone else!

One of the only negatives that I was finding from writing the blog, was that people fell silent once more — silent in terms of talking to me about Mum. Because I was being so open, honest and often upbeat in my posts, I imagine that people assumed that I was OK. I wondered whether it was time to dust off that T-shirt again.

Another problem I found was that I was becoming known as 'blog girl' and I was getting extremely concerned at how much the readers knew about me. Sometimes I would meet someone for the first time, talk to them for hours only to find out that they were actually reading my blog so they knew all the information already. I made a vow to myself not to give everything away and reminded myself that there were so many other parts of my life that people would not hear about. This was to be my 60 Postcards voice only.

I was trying to blog so often and I was meeting so many people through it that it was soon becoming like a second job for me. I could tell how much I was enjoying it because I was usually such a social butterfly and now I was beginning to turn down nights in the pub so that I could go home to blog.

I decided to take yet another massive leap of faith and do something a little crazy. I spoke to HR and my boss about taking a six-month sabbatical to focus on 60 Postcards. I had no idea what would happen but I had done the maths — I could survive financially and, besides, with more time on my hands I could put everything into it. It was worth a shot. I thought of Mum and how she would want me to do this — something that I was passionate about and made me so happy. Life is too short — I had absolutely nothing to lose. Sabbatical approved!

11

The Running Couple and Game, Set, Love Match

It was exactly four months since our adventure in Paris and I was in Broadway Market, London Fields in the east, having a leisurely stroll around the stalls with Caroline. It was a surprisingly sunny day and I was in a good place. My trip to Paris had turned everything around for me. I had a project, I had a focus — I had something to distract me from the grief that was still very much with me. I was definitely coping with it better and that was all thanks to my tribute to the person who I had lost. I had received some amazing responses from such interesting people — I felt like a very lucky girl (OK — woman) indeed.

We were having a coffee (this seems to happen so much in my life, no matter which village, town or city that I find myself in!) and while checking my emails I saw one with the subject, 'Paris 60 Postcards'. I assumed it was from one of my postcard finders replying to an earlier message. *That makes sense.*

But when I opened the email up, I couldn't believe my eyes. It was so long since I had been to Paris — this couldn't possibly be a new finder, could it? I made Caroline jump out of her skin as I shouted, 'No Way!' It was, it really was — someone else had found a postcard!

Hi Rachael

I've just found one of your postcards in the apartment we are staying in (near La Fourche Métro station) and thought it was a great idea to honour your mother's memory.

I've attached a picture of myself and my wife (Helen) picking up our numbers for the Paris marathon that we are running tomorrow. In the picture we have just realised that an error on our entry form means the country we are running for is Albania, we are in fact from Sheffield.

Dan

I read the email out loud to Caroline and we burst out laughing as we appreciated how hilarious it was that these Sheffield folk were running for Albania. What a great city to run a marathon in. These people must be super fit — *they* should be my inspiration to get into running again! I couldn't reply quickly enough:

Hey Dan and Helen,
You've made my day. My friend and I were having coffee at Broadway Market in east London and laughed a lot reading your email. You will make Albania proud I have no doubt haha! The project and blog is going very well. I'm on the move at the moment but shall reply properly when I get home this evening.

Enjoy Paris!
Rachael

Dan and Helen — hello!
How did the run go? Amazing work . . . a 10K is probably the most I will complete — I salute you!

I am still utterly gobsmacked that I heard from you four months after I left that post-card! Amazing!

So I am Rachael. I am 29, living and working in London. I always had a passion for writing and a thirst for doing something creative. It took the tragedy of Mum to motivate me and put things into action and try something different.

The blog only started a month ago but I've been overwhelmed with the amount of views and the success of social media as a spreading-it-far tool.

Here is the link (it's more a story-like blog

so have sent you the first post — you can find the rest of the posts on the right of the page). http://60postcards.com/2013/03/10/and-so-it-begins/

Undoubtedly I would love to write a post about you guys but only if that is ok with you and whether I am able to include the photo, of course. If you want to send any more info about yourselves then please do!

Best wishes to you both,

Rachael

The run went well, I finished in 3:10 and Helen finished in 3:56. It was my first run since getting a small fracture in my knee 10 weeks before in a fell race so I hadn't trained and look forward to a faster time next time. It was also a first marathon for both of us. The atmosphere was great and we both can't wait till the next one, think we have the marathon bug! The atmosphere was incredible, and having thousands of people cheer you on 'Allez Helen' 'Allez Dan' was such a boost — being able to run past sights like the Eiffel Tower was pretty inspiring as well.

Would love to see the blog to see how the project has developed.

Best regards

Dan and Helen

Hearing about Dan and Helen and their passion for running got me thinking. I used to walk home from work a lot and my sweaty, red face told me that perhaps I should leave training for a marathon until a little later in life. Watch this (very long) space. Running is a bit like Marmite, I guess. Some people *really* love it and some people *really* hate it (you know who you are, the I-left-my-kit-at-home crowd). I definitely enjoy running. I find it quite therapeutic — put your headphones in, crank up the tunes and use it as a forget-about-the-world or sort-your-life-out-in-your-head time.

I say this like I am someone who runs a lot. I don't. Not as much as I used to — not as much as I should. The most running that I have done this past year was when I outrageously decided to take on the Vertical Rush challenge with work. If you are wondering what the Vertical Rush challenge is, it's running up forty-two floors of a building (which, by the way, is nine hundred and twenty steps). It really did put those stairs at Covent Garden Tube station to shame — and I find them tough enough. Come to think of it, clambering up five floors in my office was enough. When I passed that finishing line after I had dragged my body up all forty-two floors, wondering why when I was only at floor thirteen it had felt like the seventieth, I felt a real sense of achievement. You got to down some water, take in the views and then enjoy a stuffy lift back down to the ground floor (it was quite something). I really admire runners so much for their motivation and drive to get out there come rain or shine. I must try harder — I need to take a leaf out of Dan and Helen's book! *Remember: slow and steady wins the race.*

It was so funny to think that this couple had stayed in the very same apartment as we had. They had probably been as puzzled as we were by that lectern and undoubtedly had the same wobbles up the stairs. They will have sat down for dinner around our favourite eating place — and the sunken area. Had they loved it as much as us? *Surely!* I couldn't help but wonder why it had taken so long for someone to find the postcard. I had left two there, after all, and Antoinette had said she was very busy with bookings. Still, if they were the first people to find it then I was more than happy — the surprise of such a late response made it even better.

I absolutely had to find out more about these people! I felt like this had happened for a reason because this sporting couple instantly reminded me of another perfect sporting partnership I knew a little closer to home.

Helen was born and bred in the ex-mining town of Mansfield. Apparently, as a 'true Midlander', she often uses phrases like, 'me duck', 'alreet' and 'mardy'. Well that just makes me want to pick up the phone — I love a good Northern accent! She had trawled universities up and down the country, but as soon as she visited the University of Birmingham she instantly knew that it was the right place for her and she embarked on a degree in English.

Dan was born in Leicester and grew up in a little village called Queniborough and also ended up at the University of Birmingham where he studied Medical Biochemistry. He is now a science teacher at a secondary school in Rotherham.

They explained to me that, despite the fact that they were on different courses and were in different years at university, their paths still kept crossing. When Dan had come round to collect Helen's money for the Christian Union weekend away, she had found Dan 'quite hot'. (Her words!)

Helen told me about their first date:

'Our first unspoken 'date' was at the Birmingham Glee Club to see Feist who was pretty much unknown at that point. With only 20/30 people at the gig, it was amazingly intimate — the audience sat round on

221

the floor, Dan and I sharing a bottle of wine — with that excited first date kind of feeling! Two years later we got engaged and the year after that (2007) we got married (in Mansfield). Bringing events full circle, we went to see Feist who was performing at the Glee Club the day before we set off on honeymoon. This time, however, there were several hundred people in the audience, including Dan's university housemates. Unbeknown to us, Dan's housemates had sent a message backstage to Feist telling our story — that we were newly married, that the Feist gig several years ago had been our first date and that we were about to set off on honeymoon. Imagine our surprise when during the encore Feist asked us to come up on stage to perform our 'first dance'!'

They lived in Birmingham after they were married but after a few years they were ready for a change and a new challenge and decided to head further north. Even though they had no connections with the city, they settled in Sheffield for its friendly atmosphere and the Peak District just next door. Once they had moved, they joined Totley Athletics club where Dan got into fell running and Helen preferred to stick to the roads! This sporting couple remind me so much of my parents.

My mother and father were both born and raised in Northumberland (or 'Geordieland man', as we like to call it — *still can't do the accent*). They were both from large and loving families. My dad's parents were George and Joyce and he had grown up as the second youngest of siblings Mary, Anne and Clive. They had moved from Cullercoats to Corbridge, from vicarage to vicarage, following George's job as a minister. Mum was also the second youngest of the family, growing up in Throckley with her folks, Jimmy and Peggy, and her brothers and sister, Graham, Veronica, Steve and Geoff. Because my parents were from the North, I like to think of myself as a bit of a northerner (brushing over the fact that I was born and raised in Dorset).

Living in different parts of the county, it would seem unlikely that Mum and Dad (or Viv and Paul, should I say) would ever cross paths. But they did eventually, of course, and it was because of a mutual love for sport. More specifically, it was Tynedale Tennis Club in Newcastle that brought them together. My father had been at the club for a while (club champion at one point, so I've heard) before my mum joined. My dear mother had been quite a pain at the time, apparently. Dad liked to play in the men's doubles with his mates, but Mum always wanted to play in the mixed doubles, which clashed. I asked Dad once what he had done about it. 'Well, I fancied her, didn't I? I had to do what Viv wanted!' Ah, young love. After a few months in each other's lives they became partners both on and off the court.

Now, I'm not sure my mum would appreciate me telling you this (*oops*), but my dad was a couple of years younger than her. Mum was always a little shifty about it, much to our amusement. So shifty, in fact, that we were never fully convinced of Dad's age until I found his birth certificate in his new house just last year — quite the revelation! Mum was actually four years older than him — Dad had made a few years back. *Congratulations and also apologies for never believing you.*

They played in many tennis tournaments together and one in particular had the potential to clash with a slightly more important event in their lives. They got through to the semi-finals and were faced with a quandary. If they made it through to the final, which was due to be held at the weekend, they may not make it to the church on time! It was supposed to be the day of their wedding. Luckily they lost the match (Dad likes to think they threw it — likely story) and so they had their big day at St

Andrew's Church as planned. It is a good job they didn't keep the vicar waiting, because that vicar was my Grandpa George (my father's father) who later went on to christen all of us three girls.

Dad moved all of the way down to Dorset for his first PE teaching gig at St Michael's Middle School, despite not knowing anyone in the area, and Mum soon followed, taking a PE teaching job at Queen Elizabeth's School in Wimborne, leaving her school of the same name in Hexham. After a move from Blandford Forum to Merley in Dorset, it was time for them to start a little family. That is where I am introduced to the story. *Ta da!* And poor Dad ended up with three little girls. As the only man in the house, he was subjected to temper tantrums a-plenty — 'That's *my* doll!' There was no hope of getting us to chuck a rugby ball about. I adored the way that Mum talked about having me, Sarah and Hannah. She never once complained about her pregnancies. She often reminded us that she had loved every minute, that she could have had so many more. Good job she didn't — there are only so many dress-stealing situations one family can deal with! Sarah was born two years after me, and Hannah three years after that. Apparently, I was convinced that Hannah was my own baby — you should see all of the family photos, Hannah with a terrified look on her face as I cuddle her with all of my might.

We were so immensely happy — the Chadwick gang. I feel honoured to have been brought up surrounded in such a warm and wonderful family. I guess we can all be forgiven for losing sight of this in our irrational, spotty-faced, everyone-hates-me moments as a teen. But with age I appreciate my upbringing more every day. And when your mum becomes your friend — well, that's pretty darn special. (*I'm getting a bit* Little House on the Prairie *here, aren't I?*)

My father took a second job as an LTA tennis coach so that Mum could take a break from teaching to bring us up. That break from work ended up being for about thirteen years, with a little child-minding role taken along the way to enable Mum to work from home. I am not sure I can ever thank my dad enough for enabling us to have that time with Mum — especially now, given the shock of losing her so unexpectedly and devastatingly early.

While Dad was playing and coaching on the courts, my sisters and I would go along to Mum's hockey matches. She had been a county player up North, a talented left-winger and even had a trial for the England indoor team, so she joined the Wimborne Ladies team to continue with her sport. We would sit in our bright yellow macs eating our packed lunches and cheering Mummy on.

Some people may be put off school by having parents who are teachers. But we were very lucky in that Mum and Dad never pushed us to do our homework or made us feel like we were being tested at home. They taught us to be able to get on with our work and do it ourselves and only if we didn't, would they step in.

I used to get über excited the week before school started each year. I'd try to look as sharp as possible (if only for the first day) with my fresh jumper and shiny new shoes (Clarks with the key on the sole, of course). I would beg Mum for a trip to Staples to buy a brand new pencil case and a shed-load of stationary that I *might* need. It wasn't hard to persuade her — my mum had a real (and odd) love for stationary! Now, forget iPhones, those clever eraser pens blew my mind. I would love starting a new work notebook, making sure my writing was as neat as possible. I thought it was great how your name was sewn into every item of uniform. This was soon to be replaced with yet another magic pen. It was just all too much for my excitable schoolgirl self to take.

My sisters and I would queue to wait for our hair to be done by Mum in the morning after we had eaten our cereal from the mini Kellogg's collection (so much choice). As these were times before hair-straightening tools had been invented, my curly, frizzy locks would be scraped back into a ponytail and finished off with a lovely colourful scrunchie (*gross*). Mum taught me how to do my tie properly and I had been so proud of myself when I could do it well (simple pleasures). I loved throwing my rucksack on *both* shoulders and would skip to school holding Mum's hand with a beaming smile on my face. *I was such a geek.*

I remember the excitement of finding out which of my friends were going to be in my class. I mean this was absolutely crucial to your year. I would sob if I found out that my best friend was in a different class, but soon got over it and met them in the playground to play hopscotch at break time (I know, times change). Being fickle was acceptable as a child.

School trips were just the most exciting thing in the world at the time. Oh man — I could barely sleep the night before. You'd try to work it so that you could sit near to the boy you fancied on the coach. Of course, this was the boy that you fancied on that particular week. It would be different by the next (fickle was OK then, remember). I would get my packed lunch out and pray that Mum hadn't made me egg sarnies. Please, NO! I mean, no one wanted to be the kid with egg sandwiches.

And the best thing about it all was that when the end of the school year was drawing in, I knew it must mean one thing — it was time for the family's two-week summer holiday. We went to the same place every year. There was no need to go abroad — my parents didn't want to take the three of us on a plane anywhere. No — camping in Cornwall was just right.

Even the journeys there used to be full of excitement. Dad would drive because we had a trailer and Mum was far too scared to tackle the narrow, windy roads with that thing to lug behind the car. We would have the Huey Lewis and the News cassette blasting out so that we could all have a sing-along. What I chose to do on the journeys was extremely odd indeed. Rather than play games, what I enjoyed doing was watching all of the cars fly past and trying to note down the registration numbers on a pad. I can't even tell you why I did this. Maybe I thought it would come in handy at the scene of a crime? I mean, I always knew that I was a little different but, seriously, what was that about? *Get a life — or at least a normal activity for car journeys.* And to top it all, I may never have been to Paris but I had definitely seen a certain popular landmark in my imagination on these road trips. *Children think and say the most amazing things, don't they?* As we drove along I would ask, 'Mummy, is that the Eiffel Tower?' 'No pet — that is a pylon.'

We would arrive at the campsite and I would try to do everything in my power not to help set up the tent. I hated that bit — it just seemed to take so long. Once it was up we would sort out the bedrooms. I would be sleeping next to Sarah, which always scared me somewhat — she had a tendency to kick in her sleep! I loved waking up to the sound of the whistling kettle, though, and you could hear people chattering outside. I would often get up far too quickly and smack my head on a tent pole. *Ouch.*

Over the years, we built up such a community of friends at that campsite. It was like a little summer village. We met some lovely families who we became so close to that we would plan to go back at the same time each year. These families have become friends for life, in particular the Spreadboroughs and the Chippendales (no, no — not those ones! *Now that would be a story!*). I can picture us all gathered around after dinner, Dad and his friend Pete keeping us entertained with their (terrible-but-you-can't-help-but-laugh) jokes. Mum would laugh until her eyes began to stream. *Oh, she's off again.* Before you knew it she was crying and in hysterics! Her giggle was infectious. I miss that so much.

Every year I'd look forward to hanging out with my best holiday buddy, Garry. We were thick as thieves — off on our bikes, messing about and it still irritates me to this day that he beat me at tennis every single time we played. (*I demand a rematch.*)

We'd go on trips to the beach and on outings to Mevagissey (what a name!), where we would spend all of our pocket money in the tacky seaside shops. 'Do you need to buy *another* shell?' What a ridiculous question — of course I did! We'd go for dinner at the Rising Sun in Portmellon where we'd sit and watch the waves crash over the road.

Everyone was just so content on those holidays. We'd spend hours reading, swimming in the pool or playing cards. No iPhones, no Kindles, no games consoles — just good, old, family fun. Also, if I am not mistaken, English summers always used to be hot. I am certain I used to rock a much better tan back then. In the days when getting tan lines were in — 'Check out how white my watch strap mark is!' *Cringe.* We will always look back on those breaks with such happy memories. Seaview International Campsite was one of Mum's favourite places and shall long remain one of mine, too.

It didn't take long for the sporting genes from both sides of the parentals to start to show in us. I have already confessed that I was a little bit of a geek (and not so chic) at school. I loved my classes but what I really looked forward to was the extra-curricular activities. What is it? Who cares — sign me up! Mum became driver and head cheer-leader as I took part in tennis, netball, hockey, rounders and athletics. And, you know what? Our parents never told us that we couldn't do something. They were happy for us to try it all.

In October half term, due to my dad's tennis coaching when we were teenagers, we would head off on a tennis and golf trip to Le Manoir de Longeveau in France with a large group of families. Rather than flying over, we would take the ferry and this is where the comedy would begin. Mum hated ferries. And when I say hated — I really mean it. She suffered very badly from seasickness and no tablet or weird wristband seemed to be effective enough for her. Instead my mum, hilariously, had her own way of dealing with the rocky journey that the autumnal winds would inevitably provide. She made up her own concoction of medication to get through these tricky times — it was called port and brandy. I remember trying a bit of this once — jeepers! *No wonder that cured her, it was enough to knock anyone out for hours!*

We would spend our time in France going for coaching sessions and entering all sorts of tournaments and competitions. My dad was in charge of the children's events and my mum took over as the organiser of the ladies' tennis. Due to the fact that the Loose family used to run these trips, my mum decided to name her events 'Loose Ladies', which always made us giggle. (*If only the Looses and the Chippendales had been on the same holiday!*) We would spend the evenings having big meals and BBQs and getting to know one another in the bar of the Manoir.

The girls and I have a great memory of Mum from one of those sporting breaks. We had been out playing table tennis, drinking some *bierre* and *vin rouge* and had decided to invite friends back to our gîte to carry on the evening. After about an hour, it was time for everyone to head home. As we closed the door to the last of the friends, the bathroom door creaked open. Mum had been in there the whole time but was too embarrassed to come out as she was in her pyjamas! *Poor Mum!*

With such a link to tennis, it is unsurprising that Wimbledon was a big thing for our family. Actually, my dad was playing in a county match at Wimbledon when Mum went into labour with Sarah (luckily he made it back in time). *Close call!*

When Wimbledon hit our screens it would be on in every room of our house and we would all gather as a family to watch the big Henman matches or the final that he so sadly always missed out on making. I had a crush on Pete Sampras for a while so was happy for him to win everything, naturally.

I was down at my dad's to watch the final with the family this year and I am so glad that I was. It felt strange not to watch it with Mum but, as we are a slightly nutty bunch, it was full of enough silly moments to distract us away from that. I can't tell you how many times Dad shouted, 'You HAVE to make those first serves!' I wanted to tell the coach to pipe down from his sofa! Hannah suggested the use of the underarm serve as a tactic — interesting. Not wanting to miss a minute of sunshine, Sarah decided to watch it on an iPad outside. The iPad transmission was about one minute behind the TV and she was sitting just by the door — unbeknownst to her, we could hear everything! The repetition was driving me insane! Luckily the Internet was playing up, so she had to come inside. *Good job.* We all decided that Murray's girlfriend, Kim, fully deserves a contract with L'Oréal — seriously have you ever seen such shiny locks? We discussed hat-gate — should they wear one, should they not? *Oh, now they are both wearing one — I don't know who is who.* We cheered for Bradley Cooper and Gerard Butler who were in the crowd watching. Just in the spirit of sport, of course. Not because they were looking ridiculously handsome. The funniest moment was when Hannah stood up and announced that she was going to check the BBQ. 'Hannah — sit down and shut up, it's Championship point!' *What is she doing!* And then it happened. The room erupted and we had witnessed the first male British champ in seventy-seven years. I felt so proud of Andy Murray that day. Yes — it's great for British sport. Yes — it brings the nation together. But, above all, I wish my mum had been there to see it happen. *Game, set, Grand Slam.*

Interestingly, Mum and Dad always used to tell us that we met Judy Murray and her boys on one of our summer holidays at the campsite. I was certain that must be a joke? *Judy, if you read this, please may you confirm either way — thanks.*

I will always think of tennis fondly, knowing that it was what brought my mum and dad together. I have a huge amount of respect for my parent's relationship. They really were best friends and I loved the fact that later in life they became golf partners, too. They did everything together. Not once did I hear my parents have a blazing row. A few huffs and a bit of the silent treatment here or there, maybe, but I never heard a full-blown argument. Their love was completely unconditional and they were partners in crime and advisors to each other throughout their time together. I am almost certain my mum thought Dad was the funniest man in the world. *Someone had to!*

After thirty-four years of marriage, and especially in my mother's last days, my parents seemed more in love than ever. Mum would be in the lounge telling me how much she loved Dad, how great he was being and how he was showing her why she married him. In just the next moment, Dad was in the dining room telling me how incredible Mum was and how he was blown away with how well she was dealing with everything. It was heartbreaking and beautiful at the same time. I just hope that I am able to find what they had — the bar has been set high.

They were the perfect partnership — a love match made in heaven. Hearing from Dan and Helen and being reminded of Mum and Dad made me wish for them the same kind of long-lasting relationship. I felt a real connection with the couple and looked forward to keeping in touch with them. They both added me on Twitter and told me that they were now following my story through the blog. Not only that but I found very quickly that they had spread the message to friends, as I received the following blog comment that warmed my heart:

'Helen shared a link to this story with us at work and so I started reading the blog. After reading the first couple of posts I promised myself I would catch up by reading them at the same intervals of time which you had written them, therefore not catching up and having to wait for the next post . . . Well it's 24 hours since Helen sent the link and I've read them all, am totally inspired (to do what, I'm not yet decided . . . but totally inspired!), but now desperate for the next story . . . I don't know you or your mum, but from reading and immersing myself in

your story I know your mum would be over-flowing with pride. We've already decided at work this needs to become a film! (And you have a cast of willing extras from Sheffield!)'
[Friend of Dan and Helen]

Not only was I hearing from the finders now, but also from people who knew them! This ripple effect was incredible. *How far will it go?* I was so pleased that there seemed to be a growing number of people enjoying the story as I lived it.

It was a few days after the first email from Dan and Helen that I received another message that would send me into a spin of excitement. This time, though, it was from Stephanie, the dancer in New York, again:

Hello Rachael,
Congratulations on the start up of your blog! I think it's such a perfect way to honor your mom.
So today was the day I dropped your postcard off somewhere in the city. And what better place to put it than the Shakes-peare and Co. in Soho! It was the first 70 degree, perfectly sunny day of 2013. I also happened to be with the same person that I was with when I found the postcard in Paris. I placed it on a very colorful hard

copy shelf, in between the *Jabberwocky* by Lewis Carrol and *Great Expectations* by Dickens. Classics. I sent you a separate email containing photos from my iPhone.

This week is my ballet company's New York Lincoln Center season. It marks the first time my company has performed in NYC in nine years! After this week, we start touring to other places like Florida, Washington DC, Russia and Tel Aviv.

Let's be Facebook friends, I'm sending you a request right now!

Take care (and see you soon),

Stephanie

Stephanie had not only found my postcard and had taken the time to respond to it but now she was becoming part of Team 60 Postcards! How amazing to think that my postcard was somewhere on the other side of the world waiting to be found by someone else.

Was it time for another city break?

12

Serendipity

Serendipity — a happy accident or a pleasant surprise

'OMG, are you, like, British or something?'
'Yes, darling, yes I am. Please may I have a cup of Earl Grey? Oh, gosh, how delightful!'

That's right — there was only one place to go after getting the news that one of my post-cards had flown from one side of the world to the other. I had to jump on a plane to follow it. *So dramatic!*

It was about three weeks after I had received Stephanie's first email that I had landed in New York with best friend, Caroline. Knowing that Stephanie had left the postcard in the Shakespeare and Company bookshop in the Big Apple, I felt like there was unfinished business for my 60 Postcards project. There were fifty-nine more handwritten notes that needed to be scattered around the city to join that one from Paris — and that is exactly what I would do. This was a trail too good to miss. Just as I had done in Paris, I started writing the postcards on the journey over and continued as I went along:

PLEASE READ! CONGRATULATIONS —
you have found 1 of only 60 postcards scattered
around NYC. I have left these here in memory of
my wonderful mother who passed away last
year. You are now part of the 60 Postcards
project, which started with 60 being left in Paris.
I'd love you to be a part of it and the blog that
I have created! Please email me with your name,
a photo and what you were doing when you
found it and any other stories you would like to
tell. Thank you,
Rachael x

This was another brand new city to tick off my list — another favourite from afar. The transition to New York life was wonderfully effortless for Caroline and I, and with the obvious similarities to London, this was a city that we felt we would fit into right away. And, of course, we had to stay in an Airbnb after the success of Paris — I managed to book an unbelievable corner apartment in a high rise just three blocks away from Times Square. *Sex and the City* eat your heart out. *Let me be Carrie — just for one day.*

Now I can understand why people say

London is a similar city to New York. It has the same trendy bit, the tourist haunts, the artists' hub, the yummy mummy area, the hold-on-to-your-bag parts and the financial district, of course. The only difference is that what we can do, they can do better. Piccadilly Circus is definitely a poor man's Times Square. *I'm not necessarily saying that's a bad thing.*

Using phrases like, 'three blocks away' added to the fun. *I sound so cool.* But the road numbering completely foxed me — 'It's on 203 west, between 42nd and 43rd.' *I made that up.* Numbers are really not my thing. I wondered if I would ever get the hang of it; until I looked at a map and realised that it was a grid system. *How am I so slow on the uptake?* The numbering of the streets was actually, genius. *Hang on — can we do this in London somehow? Probably a little too much work for that?*

'Do not J-walk.' What happened if you did? Would a blue-and-white police car whiz around the corner, lights flashing? *I must remember — I am not in a film.* Red hand replaced red man, and white man replaces green — and as we mastered the art of crossing the road we noticed that there were plenty of strange characters on the streets. But coming from London we were prepared for this. We merely shrugged and let out an exasperated sigh as a man strolled past us walking his cat on a lead. *Standard.*

We spent our days coffee drinking, postcard dropping, yummy-food eating and shopping (we hadn't had much time for the latter *dans Paris*). Caroline took me to Warby Parker to get some new sunglasses. *Never heard of it. I am definitely not a trendsetter.* The shop was so cool, everyone in there was a flipping fashionista and they even emailed the receipt to me for a 'paper-free' experience. As I left the store and heard my phone ping, I thought I had a new friend called Warby until I remembered what it must be! *Stop embarrassing yourself.*

I was so excited to be on the next adventure, looking back at the magic of the postcards in Paris. I had high hopes for NYC, too. Unfortunately, I was not one hundred per cent healthy — I had whooping cough. *Yes, adults can still get that — unbelievable.* It was very painful, not to mention loud (I slept on the sofa to save Caroline from the coughing all through the night) but I was determined not to let it spoil my break. My spirits were high. That was until I was confronted by, 'Mothers', 'Mums' and 'Moms' in every shop window. *How odd?* You know when something is on the forefront of your mind and it goes with you *everywhere*. It turns out that Mother's Day was approaching on Sunday. *Stop following me.*

It reminded me of the milestones and of why I started this project in the first place. I used to get so anxious before big dates and so I had chosen my mum's birthday for the tribute and Mother's Day for the release of the blog — I was turning the focus of the day on its head. Maybe it was fate doing its work which had made my trip fall on that date. There was no way I could have known, Mother's Day in the States is on a different day to the UK. Whatever it was, with my postcards firmly in my bag and an exciting night on Saturday to look forward to, I was able to browse past the Mum-covered window displays with ease. *These things cannot beat me anymore. I will not let them.*

On Saturday evening, we were off to see a show. There was no way I could travel all that way without seeing a performance. The only problem was that, as tourists, we were learning the ropes about getting around the place, as it was, and that night we were heading a little further out of town — all of the way to New Jersey. *Will we ever find the place?* Luckily, Caroline is an excellent map reader so off we set — confident with our game plan.

We took the subway to Penn Station. I forced Caroline to stop for a while as break-dancers free-styled by the platform. *I could watch this all night.* We made it to the train station with plenty of time to queue up for our tickets. It was a mighty long queue but we passed the time mainly by eavesdropping on the accents we heard around us. *When will I ever be able to do an American accent?* The ticket officer informed us that we were at the wrong side of the station. Suddenly that 'plenty of time' was slipping from our grasp. There was a tension in the air as we sprinted to the other side. *Control your breathing and, for goodness sake, try not to cough.*

We missed our train by one minute. *DON'T PANIC!* Luckily, Caroline, who along with map reading is also a transport expert extraordinaire, managed to rustle up an alternative route which should get us there in time for the show. We would be cutting it fine, but we could do this. *We have to do this!* Bish bash bosh — we were on the next train and, after a quick change, we had made it to Radburn in New Jersey. We had plenty of time to get there after all. Feeling smug, we left the station to grab a cab.

As we came out of the exit of the station we realised Radburn was not exactly what we were expecting. *Why didn't I do more research about this place?* There was no taxi rank in sight — there were no people in sight. It was a ghost town. All we could see was a petrol (correction — *gas*) station across the road. The guys in the Dunkin' Donuts shop would be able to help, though, surely? In we went and I offered to do the talking. (*What am I going to say?*) 'Oh, hello there! We seem to be a little stuck. We are off to watch a performance at Bergen Community College.' 'Oh, yeh — I went to school there. So you go up this road for a few miles then it's a left and follow it round,' the young guy replied behind the sugar-covered counter. I explained that his directions made it seem a little far for us and that we probably wouldn't be able to walk there in time. 'Wait! You don't have a car?' The shock on his face! It was as if we were aliens. (*Cheers, Sting — Now I have 'Englishman in New York' in my head. On repeat.*)

The petrol pump guy (*official title*) helped out by giving us a taxi number and then I relayed the wrong number to Caroline. *Uh oh.* Once I had managed to give her the right digits and the guy on the other end of the phone had finished his five-minute-long speech on how fascinated he was by the British accent, we had a taxi driver named Hank on his way. *Hurry up, Hank!*

Hank was twice the time they said he would be. We were now officially late for the performance that I had been so excited about in the lead-up to this trip. Feeling a little despondent, we slumped ourselves outside Dunkin' Donuts feeling like, well, complete donuts. *Dip me in caramel sauce, why don't you?*

At last (way behind schedule) we were pulling up at the incredible Anna Maria Ciccone Theatre. It was so grand — so American. As we walked up to the entrance, we were preparing ourselves for a hideous entrance involving a humiliating scramble for our seats, requiring us to climb past people apologising along the way for being the late girls. Imagine our relief when we heard that there were pre-performance speeches. *Phew.* We crept in as they were going on, slipped smoothly into our seats and, as soon as we sat down, the lights went off and the curtains began to open. *We've made it!*

The music started and the dancers began to leap on to the stage — we were at the ballet. As soon as I saw her I began to cry; I grabbed Caroline's arm and whispered, 'That's her! That is Stephanie!' I was seeing one of my postcard finders for the very first time and what better place than on stage, performing live. I continued to sob and I shook my head in disbelief. The power of that handwritten postcard in memory of Mum — just one small postcard in Paris had led me to a theatre in the middle of nowhere on the other side of the world. *I wish she could see this!* So many people had likened my real-life story to that of a film and, in that moment, I felt like I was in one. *How can this all be happening?*

Stephanie was an unbelievably good dancer. She dances beyond her years and is clearly such a huge talent. The whole show was incredible — I was in awe of the effortless poise of the company. I looked around to see the smiling faces in the audience, noticing families and feeling sad once more that my mum could not be there with me.

When I had told Stephanie by email before the performance that I was all set to come, she had asked me to wait after the show at the drinks reception so she could try her best to meet me. As the dancers joined the reception they were met by their loyal fans — all asking for photographs with them and for their programs to be signed. *Oh no — I look like a groupie! An old one, too!* Caroline and I headed straight for the free wine and chatted about the performance, while also trying to distract me from my nerves. *I hope she doesn't think I am crazy coming all of this way!*

Stephanie was one of the last of the

dancers to come out and she looked stunning in a long skirt and cropped top. *How can I compete with that?* Stephanie caught my eye and came over immediately. We hugged and I felt instantly comfortable in her presence. We chatted about the show, the Dance Theatre of Harlem, who she had been performing with and about how utterly bonkers it was that I was there because of a postcard. *Stalker alert!* She even introduced me to some of the other dancers and it was so nice to hear her introduce me as, 'The girl from London I told you about!' This was the happiest I had felt since losing Mum. This was the most magical moment of my 60 Postcards adventure so far. Not only had Stephanie become part of the project but I had a real sense that I had made a new friend.

The evening's early bout of bad luck had turned. And after chatting to Stephanie for a while longer, two of the kindest people I have met for a long time offered us a lift back to New York City — total strangers. Gloria worked in the box office at the theatre and her partner, Jon, was a light technician there. Not only did they drop us back, but they gave us a running commentary of the history of the area and tips about what to do on our next visit along the way. What a great end to a great evening.

The next morning Caroline and I ventured down from our apartment to get some coffee. While we were there I received an email that completely overwhelmed me. I broke down in tears as Caroline ushered me to a nearby seat wondering what was wrong. On the morning before the ballet we had been to the top of the Rockefeller Building and I had left a postcard at the 'Top of the Rock'. It was my New York equivalent to the Eiffel Tower and so I had worn a top with 'Paris' written on it, which had a picture of the Eiffel Tower across the front. I was so pleased to have reached the Top of the Rock, particularly as I never made it up the Eiffel Tower.

Hi Madam,
My name is Amélie, I'm a 20 years old French woman. I found this card at the Top of the Rock and I've been touch by your story. Here is the picture I made (sunny day!). Can I have the link to follow you on Facebook, please? Thanks a lot.

WHAT? HOLY — (excuse my French!) Of all the thousands of tourists to visit the Top of the Rock — of all the people from all around the world — my postcard was found by someone from Paris. And her name is Amélie! Is this a joke? From the first postcard left at the Café des Deux Moulins in Paris, to the latest postcard found by a Parisienne called Amélie in New York City, everything was coming full circle! Caroline sat in silence as the lady behind the counter at the coffee shop looked at me with pity. *OK — I've stopped crying now, love!* This had to be fate. Either that or it was my mum working her magic. *Thank goodness I followed my postcard and Stephanie to NYC!*

I met Stephanie two days after her performance and she took Caroline and I to a speakeasy bar near Times Square and she told us about what she had coming up — she was off on a world tour. *Jealous!* She even helped me slip a postcard into a menu there as we left and I told her all about my email from Amélie — she couldn't believe it. *She couldn't believe it? My jaw is still on the floor!* Caroline and I had to cut the drink short as we had a flight back to London to catch. *Don't make me go home.* But I felt sure that this was not the last time I would see Stephanie and I looked forward to our paths crossing again.

I was absolutely dreading going back to London until I remembered that I had something particularly exciting to look forward to. Lisa, a teacher from Mum's school, had been to see my dad. She had used my blog in one of her English lessons and, as a result, she had eighteen handwritten letters for me written by children in her year eight class. It brought a tear to my eye to say the least. *This is incredible.* I couldn't wait to read them. With another part of the 60 Postcards project waiting for me at home, I boarded the flight with a light heart.

When I finally got a chance to read them, I was reduced to tears — a lot of tears. All of the letters were wonderful but three of them in particular affected me greatly in very different ways:

Hi Rachael,
My name is Sorrel and we have been reading your blog in our English lesson. You first might think that's a bit weird but, this is because I am from Allenbourn Middle School in Wimborne. I was taught by your Mum in year 6 and she was a wonderful woman (wouldn't hurt a fly) and she was a pleasure to be taught by. I am now in year 8 and I can tell that this must be hard for you. What you have done has been amazing and a big impact on your life and could be for others. I would never of thought of doing anything like that and this could be very useful for me if anything happens. I am also in relation with your friend Stewart as he is

my godfather and my mum's cousin. You are an inspiration to everyone and I think what you have done is wonderful and I can't wait to read on. Take care and stay strong.

Yours, Sorrel xxx

PS Tell Stew I said 'Hi' from his god daughter.

Hello Rachael,

My name's Jordan, I'm a pupil at Allenbourn Middle School. When I was in year 6 your mother, Mrs Chadwick, taught me for English. I can't feel the pain you felt when you lost your mother, but I was so upset and shocked in fact that I had lost such an amazing teacher. I'm a term away from starting Corfe Hills now (gosh hasn't the time flown by). Mrs Chadwick will be very proud of you, for 3 different reasons, following your inspiration for being a writer. Secondly, following your heart and feeling passionate in everything you do and thirdly never forgetting she will always love you. Your mother was an inspiration to me. She was the one who always helped me with any troubles. But now she's no longer with us we all have to do things by ourselves. Mrs Chadwick would say follow your dreams. Thank you for your blog Rachael. It made me cry and realize love who and what I

have. This is me write here, right now.
Jordan

Hello Rachael,
I am Mollie aged 13 I go to Allenbourn. I knew Mrs Chadwick my English teacher and can I say what a good teacher she was. My year 6 wasn't great but having her for English always made me smile. She was that teacher you could tell anything to, like in 2006 I lost my Mum, too, 3 days after my birthday. She was helping me through it at the time. I can remember her telling me that if she ever passed away she wouldn't want her daughters to cry. She said she would want them to be happy. I love your idea of the postcards it's such an inspirational thing to do. We read your blog and it was amazing.
You're a really good writer. From Mollie

I loved the fact that Jordan quoted me by saying, 'write here, right now' from the title of one of my blog posts — what a lovely touch. And not only that but Sorrel's message was yet another sign of serendipity. Of all of the schools in that area and with all of the English classes in the whole school, it was wonderful that one of the Paris Crew member's goddaughters was in the class that was reading my blog!

Mollie's letter was very hard-hitting for me. But it was still so lovely to hear. That was just like my mum to be helping others, and I am so glad she helped Mollie. I know Mum said that she wouldn't want her daughters to cry; well, I can't say I haven't done that but it was such a lovely letter to receive. It was as if my mum was sending a message to me through Mollie.

These letters reminded me of the new angle I had taken with my blog. I had always planned to get readers involved from the outset. I knew all too well that I was going to end up rambling on and on about my own life and experiences. I did not want this to become all about me. *There is only so much that I can say without giving all of me away.* I thought about my mum and how much she inspired me when she was alive, and how her memory has inspired this incredible life-changing project. I wanted this to be a platform for others to share their own stories. I came up with the idea of 'Project Inspire'. I asked readers to send in a photo of them holding a postcard and telling me about someone or something that has inspired them, or maybe a new challenge or project that they had done. As soon as the first post went out about 'Project Inspire' I began to receive some incredible messages. I had such a great time reading them — there were people who had lost someone, people who talked about their passion for their jobs, some sent messages about being a mother. And the one that surprised me the most came from my dad:

'There was a moment years ago when we were visiting Granny and Pa in Hexham. You girls were in bed and your mum and I were having a glass of wine with Granny and Pa downstairs. An interview came on the TV. It was Melvyn Bragg with Dennis Potter (the playwright). He was very near the end of his life with cancer. It was a stunning interview and I have remembered that moment ever since thinking it would be significant for me one day.

'The thing about it was that Dennis Potter was saying as he approached the end how all the simple pleasures in life were heightened. He particularly talked about the beauty of blossom. How he couldn't help staring at it and enjoying its beauty. He had taken it for granted before.

'For me it represents the notion of enjoying as many moments as you can. Enjoy the simple yet wonderful things.'

I had never heard him speak like this before and it really touched my heart. *Pass me the tissues, immediately.*

While I was receiving these inspirational stories, and having not only seen Ballet Black perform back in February but having now met Stephanie in person, I decided to contact Cassa (the founder of Ballet Black) personally to relay the story to her and to let her know about the blog that I had created. To my delight, Cassa replied that very day and told me that if I would like to come to see the full performance of *War Letters* in Tottenham, then she would put some tickets aside for me and even offered to meet me after the show. *Sign me up!* There was no way that I was going to miss this opportunity.

I recruited Paris Crew member Clare to join me for my second Ballet Black experience, which was so lovely as Clare had never seen any ballet before — I was happy to share her first experience with her. The show was taking place at the Bernie Grant Arts Centre and we picked up our tickets and went straight to our seats. It was incredible to see the performance in full with costume and lighting and new scenes that hadn't been in the rehearsal. The skill, strength, poise, elegance and the emotion of these dancers was exquisite. Team that with some beautiful choreography and the fact that this ballet company don't just dance it, they act it and it is no wonder they are so special. *How I wish I had that talent.*

In the interval, and in true 60 Postcards style, yet another chance encounter occurred. I already felt like everything was becoming more surreal by the week and this was clearly still the case, as Clare spotted movie star Thandie Newton on the opposite side of the room. It would be great to get the opportunity to tell her all about my 60 Postcards project. She was being inundated with people asking for photos and autographs — but this was a chance too good to miss. Clare encouraged me to go speak to her and we managed to grab her attention just as the ushers were telling us to go back into the auditorium. *Just give me two minutes — I just need two minutes.*

I was stood in front of Thandie Newton (*can anyone be that beautiful?*) and I knew we had a very short space of time before the one-minute warning sounded to let us know that the second half was about to begin. This was putting my summarising skills to the test. It felt like *Challenge Anneka*. I mean, Anneka had slightly larger challenges to deal with but, still, I could sympathise with the tight timescales at that moment.

I was about to start speaking when the one-minute warning was announced. *OK, OK — we are coming.* I began to explain and it went a little like this: 'Hi, Thandie, so sorry to bother you. Mum, Birthday, 60 Postcards, Paris, Stephanie, a New York City Ballet dancer found one, Ballet Black, I saw Stephanie perform, she used to be in Ballet Black. BLOG — I'm here because of a blog, yes, but there is more, but, erm, yes, sure, POSTCARDS. Thanks so much.' *Well that went well.* I took a deep breath as I realised from her expression that perhaps it had been a little bit rushed to make any sense. But, still, she understood that I wanted a photo of us holding a postcard on the blog and she said it was absolutely no problem. The photo makes me laugh, it looks like we have known each other for years — you would never know that I had just delivered the most rushed and confusing summary of 60 Postcards to date!

Clare and I ran back to our seats and laughed at how it had gone — not so well. As we were talking about it extremely loudly, we noticed that a lady was trying to get by. Oh dear — Thandie was on the same row as us, wasn't she. I got up sheepishly to let her through. 'It's me again,' she joked as she squeezed past. I hit myself on the head with my programme at how uncool I had been, then settled down, excited to see the second half.

After the performance we stayed back at the end so that I could see Cassa, who had told me that she would meet me in the bar area. I was so looking forward to meeting her in person after a lovely exchange of emails.

She gave me a wave when she came into the room and mouthed that she would be over in a minute. She was speaking to Thandie. *I should have just waited until the end, darn it.* When Cassa came over, she sat down next to us and nattered away for a while. We talked about Ballet Black and her good friend Chris Marney, who was not able to be there that evening, and I told her all about my adventures and responses so far. I liked the fact that she was so down to earth and had a wicked sense of humour. I thought to myself that she would hopefully be someone that I would meet again in the future. What an incredible evening, all thanks to Stephanie, Beccy's mum and, of course, Cassa and her ballet company.

Now London, Paris and New York had been linked through just one postcard. This was the postcard that made me think about Mum the most. This was the one that I wanted to call and tell her about so desperately. This was the point at which I realised just how much my mum would have adored this project and how, if she had heard about something like this, she would have contacted me straight away, probably within minutes, to tell me all about it. And the fact that I had met Stephanie and seen her perform — well, it really felt like there was magic in the air and I didn't want it to end.

13

The Return

October was upon us — the days were getting shorter, the weather chillier and my life was in need of a fresh adventure. *I'm addicted.* I had been on yet another break away to Milan and Lake Como with Paris Crew member Katie and some of her friends. (*I sound like a jet-setter but, honestly, I'm not that bad!*) My bank balance was beginning to look a little on the low side but, hey, I didn't have time to worry about those things. There is a big world out there to be explored and when I lost Mum, I promised myself I'd try to say yes to any opportunities (*as long as they were within budget — just about*).

But now, my thumbs were twitching — so much had happened with 60 Postcards and I was looking for my next move. And so, on 7th October 2013 my city guide was dusted off, my beauty of a birthday camera was fully charged up and I excitedly prepared my stomach for bread and cheese once more. It was time for the return — my return to Paris.

In my new role of writer, sparked by 60 Postcards, I thought, where better in the world to get inspired than the city where it all began? I booked a last-minute, ten-day stay and, this time, I was going it alone. I wasn't as sleepy and bleary-eyed as the last time I had been pacing down Regent's Canal heading for the Eurostar Departures. *I do miss the sound of that broken suitcase, though!*

I made my way through security and passport control smoothly, and in a matter of minutes I was boarding my carriage. *I love getting the Eurostar.* And this time I found my seat in a far more mature manner. I'd even managed to scrape some make-up on to make myself more presentable. *Oh, how I've changed.* I smiled at the young man in the seat next to me as I tried to pull my laptop out of my bag in the confined space without elbowing him in the face. *Carefully does it.* I felt just a little too exposed writing on the train, though — he could see every single word that I typed. So, instead, I closed my laptop and decided to sit back and relax — listening to some tunes and trying to keep my laughing outbursts from reading Caitlin Moran's *Moranthology* to a minimum (*now that is a challenge*). The familiar sight of the 'other side' was soon in view — I felt ready to take Paris by storm. I had purchased a new French phrase book to brush up on the lingo. (Although, when I pulled it out of my bag ready to make notes, I was saddened to find that what I had actually bought was a very complex grammar book — no basic phrases in sight.) *Oh dear, this is going to be even harder than I thought.*

On arrival, with a dash of I've-been-here-before arrogance, I stormed straight for the exit and the taxi rank, assuming that I could beat the crowds. Well, you know what they say about 'to assume is to make . . . ' — the queue was about forty deep and I realised, slow on the uptake, that I was clearly not the only person who had been here before. *Never assume again.* After politely declining an offer of a motorbike ride to my destination (*I do not have a death wish, thank you*), I decided to head for a café until the queue had subsided. Three cappuccinos and far too many pages of absolutely pointless French grammar notes later (*what does this mean?*), I was in a taxi heading for the Arc de Triomphe. Google Maps had previously informed me that the accommodation I had booked (courtesy of Airbnb, once more) was 'approximately' a fifteen-minute walk from there. I had neglected to factor in my considerably hefty bag in the boot. *Cue a slow, arm-aching journey ahead.*

I made it to the flat in the 17th arrondissement and messaged the host, Herve, to let him know that I had arrived on time. (*Yes, I just said 'on time' — I even shocked myself.*) He came to the front door of the apartment block, and after a '*Bonjour*' and a double-cheek kiss we were climbing up the red-carpeted, spiral stairs to the fourth floor. I was trying to power through and pretend that I wasn't running out of breath as I scaled the endless steps. My red face told a different story. Poor Herve had kindly offered to take my bag; a decision I imagine he regretted the minute that he first lifted my ten days' worth of luggage. Well, at least I knew that I could put my running gear to one side; this was going to be more than enough exercise! *Note to self: do not leave anything behind when I go out of the apartment for fear of the stair climb of doom.*

Herve and I chatted about what we both did. I told him that I was a writer (which still felt strange to say) and he spoke about his job as a yoga instructor and his love for London, even though he had never been. I could completely relate to that with my Paris love affair developing years before my very first visit. He talked me through the lock situation for the building (which was Fort Knox style it seemed) and off he went, leaving me to unpack and settle in. *It is strange without the Paris Crew unpacking with me.*

The apartment was exactly the kind of place that I was after. It had an open lounge and kitchen, a small room with a double bed and a bathroom. It was an ideal space for much-needed writing and some good sleep. (I had not been sleeping well in the last few weeks — I am a notoriously bad sleeper.) By hour two, I felt like I had lived in the apartment for months. I pinged a text to the family to tell them that I was safe and well, and began to unpack my belongings. *Not a bad job.* I seemed to have remembered everything on my packing list. Oh no, wait — apart from an adapter, duh! With a MacBook and a phone to charge, not to mention a fringe only kept under control by the power of straighteners, this was a faux pas that needed to be rectified quickly. Off I went to explore the area. Luckily, I managed to stumble across a nearby pharmacy and, although neither of the shop workers spoke a word of English, I stuttered and stammered, using confusing hand gestures and finally managed to buy an adapter. *Good job.* I found myself leaving them in hysterics, almost chanting '*Anglais! Anglais!*' I was very tempted to join in. But no one wants to be the English girl shouting 'ENGLISH' — in French.

I got my head down early for my first night and awoke in my Parisian dwelling the next morning feeling raring to go. I received many lovely messages from friends wishing me a 'great time on holiday', but I hadn't gone there with sightseeing in mind — I was there to get working, to get inspired and to get writing. With Paris just two and a half hours from my home station, I knew I had oodles of time to come back in the future as a tourist — years to get to know this city inside out. This was something I was very much looking forward to. *I want this place to be my second home.*

I stocked up on food (and a little wine) from the nearby *supermarché* and grabbed some fresh bread from the *boulangerie* just across the road from where I was staying. As I went to make a coffee for myself, I concluded that, after a brief yet thorough search, there was no kettle in the kitchen. I found it wonderfully refreshing boiling water on a hob. (*I almost feel like a cavewoman, except I have electricity. Slightly different, I know.*)

I sat down to my laptop and checked my emails, something I used to do once a month, but once I embarked on this project it had become a daily necessity. I saw that I had a new follower to the blog who had left a comment:

> 'I only found you today Rachael but am now determined to start at the beginning of your blog and follow your journey. My daughter was lucky enough to be taught by your mum and I enjoyed her company (and sense of humour!) on a couple of school trips. She would be incredibly proud of you . . . I am and we've never met! Congratulations what a fabulous achievement.' [Blog reader]

Now this was what made me happy about the blog. It was seven months after I had published my first post but I was still getting a wonderful message like this about Mum. *I wonder if this reader really will catch up — there is a lot to get through with my ramblings!*

I realised it was about time that I prepared a draft for my first blog post from Paris. But as I settled down charged and ready to get writing, it took just one text from Dad to bring me back down to earth with a thud. Granny (Dad's mum), the only grandparent still with us, had taken a turn for the worst. I suddenly felt very far away from home, like I was in the middle of nowhere and completely alone — just as I had done when my sister first called me with the news Mum had fallen ill. *I'm lost.* I called Dad immediately. My granny was ninety-four years old and, although her mind had been very much in full force, it was her body that was giving in. She was in Hexham, Northumberland, and Dad insisted I continue in Paris, as there was nothing that I could possibly do. I felt helpless. But I carried on, just as Dad had suggested, not wanting to let him, or anyone else for that matter, down.

The next day I decided it was about time I ventured further afield. I covered some serious ground. My mind was filled with thoughts about Granny, my dad and the girls. I needed some fresh air and thinking time. I walked past the Arc de Triomphe (deciding against a selfie) and strolled down the Champs-Élysées, avoiding the temptation of the designer stores. *Someday I will have the dollar for that.* It was as I walked through the Jardin des Tuileries that I bumped into an older American gentleman named Christopher. He had stopped me, pointing to a map, and asked me *en français* for directions. On the realisation that I was English, not only could we piece together his movements to the Métro succinctly (*I remember where things are!*), but we could also have a good chat. I got the feeling that we both needed it, two aliens in Paris; we were able to unleash our stories on each other in full. He described the time, twenty-odd years ago when he had made the brave move to Paris for love, following a girl that he had fallen for. *I'm hooked.* When the relationship hadn't worked out, he made the decision not to return to America and had travelled around Europe as an artist ever since. I admired his free-spirited, friendly nature and when we went our separate ways, we wished each other good luck for the future. I couldn't keep the big grin off my face as I walked away. *This is why I am here on my own; this is why I am doing this project.* Who else will I meet along the way?

I carried on through the Jardin des Tuileries, past the Louvre and had a pit stop in the very same café where we had stopped on our visit last December, which was aptly named Le Café de Thé (or not on this occasion, as I ordered a *café au lait*). Out came my laptop and I began to make notes on my trip so far, uploading my photos and I got completely lost in my own world through writing, as I so often do. It was only an hour and a half later when I looked up from my screen that I remembered where I was and noticed the darkness setting in outside. The waiter asked me in French if I would like anything else, but I had received a text message — it was time for me to move on.

My trip to Paris that week had coincided with that of a good friend's from home. Danny and his colleagues were over on business and he had sent me a message inviting me to join them for a drink that evening. They were in Bercy Village, which, despite seeming pretty far away on the map from where I was, would at least give me plenty of time to stroll along the Seine. As I got further along the riverside, I realised it possibly wasn't the safest route a girl should take alone. *Lesson learnt.*

I arrived at Bercy Village — it was like no other area I had visited in Paris so far. It was paved with stone and arches led into a street of boutiques, pubs and restaurants. I checked my phone about three times to check the name of the pub, struggling to see it on the busy street. I made it (*it shouldn't have been that tough*) and on meeting them all I was glad to have drinks with some fellow Brits. I may have only been in Paris for two days, but I really appreciated being able to have a full-flowing conversation. *I really need to brush up that French.* It didn't take long for the drinks to start kicking in. It was time to grab a taxi home and I found out the hard (and expensive) way that there was another street name very similar to the one that I was staying on. *Serves me right for drinking too much.* Annoyingly, it happened to be on the opposite side of the city. *I must say the arrondissement number next time, muppet.*

The next morning, Thursday, due to a slightly sore head (self-inflicted misery is the worst), I spent the day taking it easy, only leaving the house once for a quick coffee and a restock of food from the shop. Even that was a little too much for me to cope with! *Ouch.* I had a slow day of writing and reassured myself that tomorrow would be a new day. *Why do today, what you can do tomorrow?* On Friday morning, I walked to Montmartre, a place that held so many fantastic memories from our December trip. I planned to walk by the Café des Deux Moulins, the *Amélie* café, and perhaps stop for a coffee. I knew I was in roughly the right place, the streets looked very familiar, but for some reason I began to doubt myself. I asked a super-friendly French man, who introduced himself as Robert, for directions. He said that he would walk me to the street the café was on in return for letting him practise his English on me. *You have got yourself a deal.* We stopped by the Montmartre Cemetery, as it was on the way, and Robert showed me the grand gravestones of two famous French national treasures. One was Émile Zola, an influential French novelist, and the other was a popular singer called Dalida, who had tragically committed suicide aged fifty-four in the late eighties. I would never have known that these were here without my personal tour guide. As we approached the street that I was after, we thanked each other and went on our separate ways. He had become another character in my story.

The *Amélie* café was packed to the brim, no room inside or out. But the café wasn't going anywhere and I promised myself to try again another time, and so I set off up the hill to the Sacré-Coeur, following exactly the same path as we had as an eleven-strong group. I couldn't help but chuckle to myself as I reached the top in just ten minutes. That walk had taken hours last time around! My mind flashed back to dancing with the buskers as I passed the spot where they had performed. *Good times.* I wandered around the cobbled streets, stopping to buy some postcards (*what a shocker!*) from a little souvenir shop and treated myself to a delicious cheese and ham crêpe. *Bethan would love this.* The Place du Tertre — the artists' square — was buzzing with painters, locals and tourists. People sat all of the way around the outside having a coffee or a glass of wine. *I'm jealous.* I felt like I could quite happily spend the rest of my days there. An artist approached me to ask if I would like a painting of myself. I was shoving a crêpe in my mouth as he asked and I was red-faced after my hill climb — why would I want a picture of myself? *I do not want a memory of my face like this. Or at all, thanks!*

I headed for the steps at the Basilica and was saddened to find the football-performing busker was missing from the lamp post. *Come back!* For some reason, I had naively assumed that everything would be as I left it in December, forgetting that in ten months life was bound to move on. I took some snaps of the breathtaking view across the city attempting to beat the ones I had taken before (*no chance — I only had my iPhone*), finished my crêpe and headed back to the square, slipping in and out of tourists like the Artful Dodger to avoid 'the artist'. *No — I still don't want a painting of myself, sir.*

I took a seat outside a bar and ordered myself a (large) red wine. I started to get my laptop out but suddenly realised that this was not the place for such things. It was an inspiring and creative space — I decided that my notebook and pen would be a much better fit. I felt more productive than ever, words flowing as I fed off the enlivening environment around me. This had been my favourite day so far and I took my time wandering back to the apartment, stopping for a wine on the way where the waiter didn't even realise that I was English until I paid. *No way. He thought I might actually be French!* What an end to a delight of a day. And, to top it off, I was excited about tomorrow — I had a visitor arriving.

Just before twelve the next day, I received a text message from my dad. 'Hi Girls. Granny just passed away peacefully in her sleep. Love you all, Dad.' As Dad and I spoke on the phone, we soon found ourselves talking through tears. I was so sad for my dad, knowing what it felt like to lose my own mum. I was angry, so angry that this was happening to him so soon after what had happened to Mum, too. Losing your wife and mother in only one year and eight months was just not fair. *It is never fair, regardless of the timescale.* What made it even more difficult was that, as he explained the process of what was now happening with Granny — that her body was still at home and that they were waiting for the undertakers — he stopped suddenly, realising and acknowledging that I was all too familiar with the form. 'It's a bit raw for us, isn't it?' he said.

Absolutely. I know that my granny would understand me feeling this, but all that was filling my head in that moment were memories of the time Mum had gone. Dad insisted I stay in Paris until he had further news — that it was what Granny would have wanted. I now had another inspirational woman to do this for and I was determined to compose myself and to keep going.

A few hours after I had received the sad news (and with perfect timing), my best friend Caroline arrived at the apartment. It was her birthday and she had come over to join me for a few nights to celebrate. I met her on the ground floor and gave her a health and safety briefing before the mountain climb that she was about to face up the dreaded stairs. In true Herve style, I offered to carry her case up (oh, wow — it hurt). We walked into the lounge. 'It's perfect!' Caroline exclaimed on her first look at the flat. I had bought some pretty pastries to put on the wooden workbench along with a postcard and a present. I even lit some tea lights for her to blow out for the full birthday effect.

We decided to head straight out for some food and a catchup. I told Caroline about the sad news and promised her that we would celebrate in style and we would, of course, raise a glass to my wonderful granny. We sat down for lunch. It always made us laugh how we could not see each other for only a few days but still talk for hours and hours about every little detail of what had happened since. I couldn't have been happier to see her. With food and catch-up done, it was time to head back to the apartment, put on some music, open a bottle of *vin* and get into our dresses and heels for the night ahead!

As we headed out for the Métro (heels now in bag and flat shoes on — a sign of getting older, comfort over stilettos any day), we stopped off for a drink and ended up in a deep conversation about Mum and about the time that we lost her. Caroline was one of the only people in the world that I felt I could really go back to this traumatic time with. She made me feel at ease, never letting me feel guilty for a second for speaking from the heart — from my broken heart. We chinked our glasses and cheered, '*Salut!*' to the people who were no longer with us and jumped on the underground to St Michel in central Paris. Birthday girl had expressed a craving for a steak dinner, so that is exactly what she would get. We had a comical chat with a waiter — both Caroline and I determined to speak only French (which went well for us, not sure the waiter agreed!). We couldn't see an option for a glass of wine so, naturally, we were forced to buy a bottle. Delicious dinner was devoured and we were off to a jazz bar just across the street. Caroline was a singer in a band back home, The Interiors. I was one of her biggest fans and groupies. She always talked about her dream of performing in a jazz café in Paris one day. We walked into Le Caveau de la Huchette, somewhere recommended by not only the Paris guide, but a friend, too. It was even more magical than we imagined. *Caveau*, meaning vault, was exactly as its name suggests! The stone basement was filled with hot bodies, twirling to the jazz music — the soulful band of trumpets and a see-through piano finished with a husky-sounding front man. Caroline had a birthday dance with a gentleman three times her age, which I stored as ammunition for future teasing. We gushed about how wonderful a night we'd had all the way home in the taxi.

Sunday brought hangover number two of my stay and this time I was pleased I had a friend to wallow with. Delirium kicked in as we noshed on our *croque monsieurs*, reminiscing about the magical evening we had experienced. We took exactly the same route as I had done just a couple of days before from the apartment to the Louvre. I was starting to feel like a local, despite the fact that it was just a walk down one straight road — not the toughest route to remember! When we approached the Louvre we decided we needed a photo taken. (I had been on my own before and realised there was no proof I had actually been there!) We asked a fellow tourist who gave us a mini heart attack when we handed her the phone and it looked like she was putting it into her bag to walk off. We were preparing for a chase when we realised she was just putting her scarf away. *Well, that could have been awkward!*

That evening, I had a surprise for Caroline but I wasn't going to reveal the details until later. We continued on to Notre Dame where we were lucky enough to catch a glimpse of the ministers in full robe, gathered outside the back of the cathedral, waiting to go in for a service. Just a little further along the river was the Love Lock Bridge (or Pont des Arts). Not having had a chance to leave a lock at the bridge was my one and only regret of my previous visit. Unorganised as ever, I was without a lock so we went to the nearby souvenir shop to buy one and borrowed a Sharpie pen to write on it: 'Viv, Mum. I love you xxx'

It wouldn't be right if I didn't leave a postcard alongside it. A postcard that I was well aware would only be for me. Lost in the sea of locks and with the potential for damage by rain, it could well be destroyed within a day. Still, I left my heartfelt message:

> Mum this lock is for you. I think about you every day and wish I could have taken you to Paris. This lock is left with more love than you could imagine. I am going to make you proud. I love you, Rachael xxxxxxxxxxxxxxx 60postcards.com

I felt emotional — this lock was made for lovers but my love was of a different kind. The unconditional love of a daughter for her mother. I decided right there and then to make a note of where my lock was and vowed to try my best on every future visit to go back there, to claim my lock to keep as a souvenir and leave another to last until next time. *Now just don't lose those keys!*

I said goodbye to the bridge and, with Caroline trying to keep me calm, we found ourselves outside the Shakespeare and Company bookshop. It was my first visit and it did not disappoint. I was giddy with chatter, telling Caroline over and over, 'This is where Stephanie was, she was right here!' Conscious of my repetitive ramblings, we went into the literary cove, winding our way past bookshelves aplenty. We went up to the second floor to find the piano room. I slumped on the sofa as, without me even noticing, Caroline took her place at the piano playing for the visitors. I wrote some postcards and left them in various cubbyholes, noticeboards and secret spots. This time I wrote: 'You won't believe what happened in this book-shop . . . ' On the way out I was lucky enough to grab one of the staff to tell him my story. Excitedly, he took a postcard with my details on, with a promise to check out my blog. *I still can't believe what happened here myself!*

I had been given instructions of where to find the evening's birthday dining surprise for Caroline. You see, this was not your regular restaurant. We would be having dinner in someone's home — a stranger's home. (As I write this I realise that it sounds far more dangerous than it was!) We headed under-ground to the Alésia Métro station and followed the step-by-step instructions (which even included the amount of paces for each stage of the journey). We got to the giant green gate and entered the passcode, as instructed. I hesitated in a moment of fear. What if this was a scam? What if this was not as I thought? I rechecked my emails and calmed myself — I had done plenty of research beforehand. The door clicked open. We were definitely in the right place.

As we swung open the gate, Caroline and I

looked at each other — saying nothing — giving each other a reassuring nod. We were at the house of Jim Haynes for one of his Sunday night dinners.

Caroline first mentioned these to me around four years ago and I have spotted the odd article or two about them online since. Even when she first mentioned longing to go, I never forgot — I just needed an opportunity. And her birthday weekend seemed the ideal time. Seventy-eight-year-old Jim has been opening up his house for locals and tourists alike every Sunday evening for the past thirty-odd years, asking for no fee, simply a donation to go into arts funding. Jim was born and raised in Louisiana, USA, coming over to London and Edinburgh in the seventies to set up the Traverse Theatre Company. A like-minded soul, he has a real passion for meeting and introducing new people. These social soirees are an opportunity for people from all around the world to gather together. We were in heaven.

Now, these may have started as small dinner parties, but over the years they had developed into huge gatherings, with Jim hosting up to seventy people at one time. To cope with increasing numbers, Jim gets a chef in to cook for his guests every week. We went into the crowded, artistic, open-plan front room, squeezing past strangers who were spilling out on to the terrace.

It wasn't difficult to spot Jim — having already read reviews that described him sitting at a high stool next to the kitchen area with an apron on clearly stating his name. We stood nervously waiting to introduce ourselves. He welcomed us, crossed our names off the guest list and urged us to help ourselves to food and drink. It was stew to start followed by a hearty beef dish with deliciously roughly mashed potato and fresh green veg. The wine and beers were lined up on the side bench — an unlimited supply. (I groaned to myself as I realised I was still suffering from the night before. *Take it easy.*)

The first people we met were a lovely lady named Ike, from Germany, and New Yorker Stuart. All we needed was that first conversation for us to relax and, before we knew it, we were chatting away as if we had known these people for years. Stuart is a lawyer who had recently made the move from New York to Dalston in London. We were excited to hear this and promised Stuart, who explained he knew very few people in London, that we must meet up on our return home to take him out and show him the sights.

Di was the next person that I conversed

with. Originally from New Zealand, Di now lived in Antwerp with her daughter and granddaughter, who followed her there and lived in the flat above. Di was such a bubbly character with a wicked sense of humour — we hit it off immediately. She surprised me when on asking if she did her photography in Antwerp, she announced that she actually ran photography courses in Lake Genoa, Italy. Well, of course! She was just in Paris on a short stay and introduced me to a lovely lady, Sarah — someone who knew Di from attending her course. Sarah had just moved to Montmartre from Ohio and had decided to make the change from her previous job of running art galleries to embarking on a new venture setting up her own jewellery range. When she asked me what my story was and why I was there, she welled up as I told her about Mum and my project. She was the same age Mum was when she died and she said it made her think of her children. I had no idea she was that age, she looked in her late thirties. The mood was lightened when I asked her for her beauty secrets (*exfoliation is the key apparently — noted*).

One of the most beautiful moments of the evening was when Caroline and I were sitting opposite each other, each of us talking to a man who was well into their seventies. Eric, who I was sitting with, was another New Yorker who, after a career in politics, had headed south to retire in Texas. He tries to visit Paris for a month every year and, with a love for singing and music, always tries to book in performing at jazz bars around the city. Caroline was talking to Michael, the author of a perfume bible in its thirtieth edition. We both realised later that we had spoken about each other so much to them that we should have swapped — there was just not enough hours in the evening.

Jack was a very cheeky chappy. The first thing that he said to Caroline on finding out where she was from was that Aberdeen had the highest statistics for rainfall and suicide. Charming! He had gone to Kings University in London, as had Caroline, and they found they had mutual friends. The world becomes smaller yet again.

Gorgeous Emily from Toronto, Jack's partner in crime, was a joy to be around. She is a journalist and blogger. She had lived in Paris for two years and her housemate at the time had introduced her to Jim's dinners. Her cousin was at the dinner, too. She was making videos throughout the evening, ones we are slightly concerned about watching . . .

Emily told me about how she and Jack had met:

Picture this — a Canadian-American-Iranian lady falls for an English-Welsh man in Munich, Germany, a few days before Christmas. One lives in London and the other in Paris, soon to be returning to North America. And so begins the romantic journey of a long-distance couple finding their place in the world.

Jack and I met four years ago in Munich on a beer tour! The tour ended in the famous Hofbräuhaus, where we spent hours chatting, laughing and enjoying each other's company. A year later, we found ourselves backpacking through Sub-Saharan Africa together. Four years later (and now engaged!), we are continuing to take on the world, one adventure at a time.

Joelle from Paris was lovely. We got the giggles as the place got so busy we were struggling to understand each other as the noise was building. I felt comfortable with her. So much so that I had a moment when I asked her opinion on whether I needed to fix my red-wine mouth. (I was considering heading to Jim's bathroom to borrow some toothpaste but decided against it. That was a step too far, even if I was a guest in his home.)

What an incredible night we had. I had the

urge to visit Paris every single Sunday just so that I could meet more people every week. Travelling back to the station with new friends Jack, Emily and Stuart was lovely. This was what life was about and what my project was about.

On Monday we went to the street in Montmartre where 60 Postcards all began. Antoinette and I had been in touch on email a few times since our stay at her apartment. I would have loved to return to that house on my return to Paris, but I knew it would be far too large and pricey for just me. I contacted her before my visit, though, and asked if she knew of anywhere else that I could stay around the same area. I was so surprised when she offered me the chance to go and stay as a guest in her studio. I was more than delighted to accept — I couldn't wait to get back to that street again. On the morning after Jim's Sunday night dinner (cursing ourselves for drinking too much, yet again) it was time for us to pack up and say goodbye to Herve's flat. After descending the stairs of doom one last time (*wow — this still hurts*), we were off in a taxi heading for the cobbled road in Montmartre where 60 Postcards all began.

Caroline and I went to meet her on the Monday morning. It was so lovely to see her.

She was just so friendly and welcoming, as usual, and asked me all about my postcards adventure. I told her about the responses and what had happened since I had last been in Paris, and she said that she thought it was wonderful. When I told her that someone had picked up a postcard from her apartment, she nodded and smiled and said 'Good'. I then explained that it had been four months after we had stayed there and was surprised that it had been found such a long time later.

Antoinette then explained that she had been my accomplice and I didn't even know it! She had actually been the one to find the postcard in the house — she was tearing up as she spoke. She said that as she was a similar age to my mother and had children of her own, she just found it far too emotional to be able to put together any kind of response herself. It was too much for her. And so, as the host of the house, she wanted to wait to see what kind of people were staying there to see if they would seem the kind to get in touch. When Dan and Helen arrived, she said that they seemed so lovely she had no doubt they would find it. It was in that moment that I was reminded how kind strangers can be. It puts your faith back in humanity. I would never have known if Antoinette had got rid of that card or if she had kept it forever. But she wanted to help me with my tribute — she had become a part of Team 60 Postcards and I hadn't even realised it.

She asked if I was free to have drinks with her that Wednesday evening as she wanted me to meet her friend — an English lady who lived on the same street. It sounded great — I couldn't make enough friends in Paris!

Caroline and I decided to head out to Le Marais that evening and have a nice chilled dinner before she was to head home the next day. We found a place that was in a lovely courtyard with a heated area for us to sit in. Well, it was an interesting meal in the end — there was a mouse on the floor. Picture both of us stomping our feet to make it go away while we ate our food. *It is slightly distracting having Mickey bloody Mouse hanging around our feet.* We decided we'd had enough excitement for one evening and had an early night.

The next day we returned to the Café des Deux Moulins and managed to grab a seat. I was meeting a new friend there — Amélie — the girl who had found my postcard at the Top of the Rock in New York! I was bringing my 60 Postcards adventure back to exactly where it started. The first postcard I had ever left was at the *Amélie* café, now I was going to meet Amélie in that *Amélie* café, because she had found a postcard in NYC. *I am definitely in a film now — where are* The Truman Show *camera crew hiding?*

As Amélie was from Paris she was able to help me with something while we were there. You see, I had never been able to get back in touch with Alexandre who had found my first postcard there. I was so disappointed that he had got away. He had said in his message that this was his local bar and so I wanted to see if anyone recognised his name. The waiter explained that there had been a whole new turnover of staff but there was one man inside the café who might know him. My friend helped me translate the story. Sadly, he didn't know who Alexandre was but he agreed to keep a postcard behind the bar in case he ever showed up. *I still haven't heard anything, but it was worth a try. Everything is worth a try.*

Caroline left for the station and Amélie went back to her studies. I was off to meet another good friend who was over from London on business for a meeting. Roland and I met at the Printemps shopping centre and we went up the escalators to the top floor. Wow — what an incredible view. You could see everything — so much more than from the steps of the Sacré-Coeur with the perfect 360 view. We had a catch-up and moved on to another bar, as I told him everything that had happened over the past week and how I had met Amélie earlier that day. As we said our goodbyes, I realised in that moment that I really was in no rush to go back to London. I felt like Paris could quite easily turn into a second home. It has given me so many happy memories. I love Paris more than I ever thought I would.

On Wednesday evening it was time to meet Antoinette and Luan. Antoinette had asked me to pick up some snacks. She must have thought I was slightly crazy when I replied saying, 'What exactly do you mean by snacks?' I went to the *supermarché*, loaded a bag with cheese and chorizo, oh, and some tomatoes and crisps and hummus and a few other things, just for good measure. *I know I have gone overboard — better to have too much than too little.*

I went ahead to Luan's flat, as Antoinette was going to follow a little later. As I got to the front door and knocked loudly I heard frantic yapping. Ah, she had warned me about the dogs. Luan welcomed me in and laughed as I unpacked my Mary Poppins bag full of treats. *Yep — I have definitely gone completely overboard.* I had a beer and sat down with the dogs jumping with excitement at the new person in the house as Luan put together some nibbles. *I'm not used to dogs — act cool.*

Luan was a fascinating lady and such fun to be around. She is currently spending a year out while setting up a design venture specialising in gifts for new fathers. She recently won two national innovation and design prizes for her patented aquatic baby carrier and is now in the process of raising funds and convincing investors to back her invention so she can make a quick buck, retire early, buy a farm and rescue more dogs.

Before inventing, Luan spent 15 years as a communications expert in a Parisian PR agency and a French environmental multinational. She was a spokesperson, crisis management expert, branding consultant and bungled her way through many hairy situations, many of which happened in China, where she regularly travelled for work. And the part that was most interesting to me was that she is a published children's author. This is why Antoinette had wanted us to meet. As a writer, she kindly thought that Luan may be able to give me some advice on books and being an author. It was a great help and I excitedly showed her some of my writing as Antoinette arrived.

Antoinette told me about the history of the

road that they lived on. In the sixties it had been a mews with craftsmen's studios and repair shops before turning into a residential area. In the eighties it became a mixture of residential homes, art schools and web companies. But in the nineties it was threatened with demolition so the residents and artists came together to create a petition to keep it from being destroyed and, thankfully, they won!

When I said to Antoinette that her house had reminded us of a film set when we stayed there in December, she said that it had in fact been used for filming! There is a house party scene near the end of the romantic comedy, *2 Days in Paris* featuring Julie Delpy and Adam Goldberg where Antoinette's house makes an appearance. A television programme *Design for Life* had also been filmed there. It was a BBC reality TV documentary which saw twelve young designers compete in an *Apprentice*-style competition. The lady who won was from England and apparently Antoinette had also taken her to meet Luan. I had a lovely evening with the ladies and I was glad that I now had two friends on the street where it all began.

I got a taxi to the Gare du Nord after saying goodbye to Antoinette the next morning and I had a real sense that she had become more of a friend now, rather than a host. As I got the Eurostar home I took out my notebook, Mum-style, and scribbled down everything that had happened and everyone that I had met. There was so much to write that I ended up scribbling like a maniac and my writing was barely legible. We pulled up at King's Cross and, as I got off, I felt sad to be home. I was even more sad at the thought of attending Granny's funeral in just a few days' time.

★   ★   ★

On the day before the funeral, I embarked on what became an absolute nightmare of a journey to the North East. It is a journey that is supposed to take four hours max. It ended up taking more than seven hours — great. King's Cross was full to the brim with irate passengers after hearing the news that all East Coast trains to Newcastle had been can-celled. I headed off to Euston station to give the west route a go — trying to take deep breaths as I went in order to keep my anger levels from rising too high.

I found out that I could get the Glasgow train to Carlisle — things were looking up. Well, they were looking up until I reached the platform. Clearly the rest of the world was doing the same thing. I got on a carriage and looked down it in despair. It was packed and I had a huge bag with me — I had no chance. I was either going to have to stand or sit on the floor. A father and son jumped on the same carriage and explained that they were in exactly the same predicament as me. The dad suggested we try First Class until we got chucked out. I was game: 'If you do it, then so will I.' So off we got and dashed down the platform with just two minutes before the train was due to depart. We snuck into the luxurious carriage, enjoying the comfy seats and masses of leg space. It felt a bit naughty — but, really, we had no choice. The dad turned to me and asked what my game plan was. They were from Australia and joked that, being from the other side of the world, it gave them the right to 'play dumb'! I explained that I had no game plan but that I wasn't going to move! I simply showed my ticket to the conductor, who looked at it and carried on. The same happened to the others. (By this point, I had picked up that the little boy's name was Charlie but the dad's name was still just 'Dad'. I was too far into the journey at this point to ask.) Charlie looked at me and, when out of the sight of the conductor, he punched the air while mouthing 'Yes!' Happy days. First class it would be. (What I haven't mentioned was that this train broke down approximately one hundred and fifty yards into the journey. For 27 minutes. Classic.)

I changed at Carlisle and *finally* got to Wylam (where we were crashing at my uncle and aunty's house) to meet Dad. It was only when I spoke to Dad that evening that he told me about the last conversation that he'd had with Granny on the phone. His two sisters, Mary and Anne, had been with his mum in Hexham and they had sensed that she was in her final moments. They felt like she was holding on and so they called my dad so that he could speak to her. Granny wasn't able to talk at this point but, still hoping that she would recognise his voice, he told her all the latest news, including the news about my blog and an update on the 60 Postcards story. I was so pleased that he got to say goodbye. And now I was even more determined to keep this project going for my family.

We got up very early in the morning and met all of the family at the church, including Sarah and Hannah, who had stayed at Sarah's friend's house in Newcastle. I was so happy to see them and I wanted us all to be together for following the coffin into the Abbey. We all knew that this day was going to be particularly tough, given that it was the first funeral since Mum's. The coffin, the service and the hymns (two of which were the same as at Mum's) just brought everything back. And I think that it made everything feel so much more real — I couldn't hold it together this time around and that proved just how much shock I must have been in last year. It was a beautiful send-off for Granny, who was such a strong, supportive, caring and inspiring lady. She had been like a mum to our mum, and Dad told me that he wished Mum had been there to say goodbye. We got through the day and spent time with the family in the evening. I was happy to have that extra night with Dad — Hannah and Sarah had gone home by this point — and was able to drive him back down to Dorset in his car so that he could rest. He was exhausted. Once again, it had all been too much.

After a week at home I headed back up to London and I was excited about a night I had planned with Caroline and two new friends. We couldn't believe it as we sat with Stuart and Jack from Jim's Sunday night dinner in Paris. Here we all were in London together. We spent the night laughing our heads off, especially as we were giving Stuart slightly false information about British culture as a bit of a joke. We told him that pantomime was a chance for the audience to dress up — but only the men — and that they have to go in drag. We told him that we would take him at Christmas. *I cannot wait for that!*

It had been a roller coaster few weeks but I was feeling positive about the months ahead. I was doing this for Mum and for Granny. Nothing was going to stop me now.

14

The Show Must Go On

I am currently sitting in the Booking Office Bar in the spectacular King's Cross Renaissance Hotel. It has proven to be one of my favourite mobile office spaces ever since I first set foot in there. I have been able to enjoy the breaks from writing by looking out of the window to see the Eurostar arrivals: the suited and booted workers returning from their business meetings, the tourists clutching their souvenir bags, the friends chattering away about their adventures, the families herding their children along the platform and my favourite — couples reunited in a romantic embrace. Looking out of the window at the Eurostar leads me to reminisce about my two wonderful adventures in Paris — a city that, in my heart, will now and forever belong to my mum.

I feel lucky to live in this part of town — such a transient part of the city but also so homely, too. I feel like a local, especially with all of this time to spend my days writing. My favourite place in the whole of the station is the piano just near to the departures for the Eurostar. The piano sits and waits for people to come and play — passers-by, pensioners, children and I have even seen people practising for their lessons there. My favourite of them all was a man named the Modern Day Jester. He would play while beat-boxing and singing along. I had to text my mum as soon as I heard him. People watching and listening to music were things she loved so much. I never took her there. *I wish I had taken her there.*

When I decided to take my sabbatical from work to focus on my writing, I soon realised that this would be the first time in my working life that I would be going it alone. I have been so used to working as part of a team in so many aspects of my life — I thrive on bouncing ideas off others — and so, naturally, I wondered how lonely I would feel with just me, myself and my MacBook.

In the beginning stages I really did miss being around other folk. But, as time went on, I realised that, just as I had found on my return to Paris, being on your own throws you into situations and gives you a chance to meet people that you would never have met if you were a part of a group. I have spoken to so many friendly waiters, shop owners, bar staff and fellow customers, and now interaction with people is back in my routine. And, not only that, the 60 Postcards project was always supposed to be for more people than just myself. I wanted it to be *Team 60 Postcards*. Because so many people were following and supporting my story, and with my friends and family in touch all of the time asking for updates, I found that, actually, I was probably less alone than ever before! This blog comment, in particular, showed so many links through both loss and my postcard locations:

'Morning Rachael (it's very early here in Glasgow!), I have been following your story since about April. I find many parallels with you and can empathise, you are doing a good job here — I too lost my mum some six years ago, but when I was a student I had spent a quite special time with her in Paris. I am a teacher and as I am a big time traveller I always sent POSTCARDS back to her (I have kept them as they are quite hilarious)! One of my favourite words is serendipity! Though one of my pupils told me to go to NYC this summer, I never managed it. Well, you can't pack everything in to a trip to New York — definitely next time. I try to get to Paris (Christmas) and

When I began my sabbatical, and started writing in earnest, it became clear within a few days that there was simply no knowing when was best to write. It depended a lot on my mood or, in particular, how I was feeling about Mum. Some days I found that I would wake up at six o'clock in the morning, while on many nights I would be so engrossed in writing that I wouldn't realise the time until it was four o'clock in the morning. Of course, being able to reminisce about the magical memories has been a blessing. But, as well as writing about those wonderful times, I have been forced to relive the traumatic ones, and that has been more harrowing than I could have imagined. Writing about the days I watched my mother dying was brutally tough on the heart and I don't plan to go back there again anytime soon.

Unlike the challenges facing a fiction author, my imagination does not need to be tapped — this is a true story. *My postcard tales still feel like fiction even to me, though.* I am actually experiencing the very personal feelings that I describe and the details of the events are all scattered in my head. It is a

302

matter of translating those thoughts on to the page — on to the screen. There are certain parts of my story that I am unable to read back without tears. I wonder if I will ever be able to. *Maybe one day.*

I am so content to be writing. And it's not just any writing job — it is one that involves spending all day, every day thinking and speaking about my mum. Embarking on a project that I am so emotionally invested in has resulted in me getting up every day and working my socks off and feeling so satisfied that I am finally doing something that I love. I have never felt so passionate about anything as I do about 60 Postcards.

Sometimes it still feels like yesterday that I lost Mum — other times it feels like a lifetime since I saw her smiling, heard her laugh or had the chance to tell her to her face that I love her. It was all just so quick. Looking back, those sixteen days are all a blur. I find it so difficult to piece together exactly what happened and when. It is like when someone talks to you too quickly. You pick up on the main points but the rest is lost and you have to ask them to repeat everything again. But there is no way for me to do that with my situation — there is no way that I can make sense of all the details during that traumatic time.

Some people have said that writing about it all must be some kind of alternative therapy for me — that is most definitely true. But regardless of that, nothing will ever take the pain away of what I have felt or of what I am still feeling. Mum was such an incredible person — I can't begin to comprehend why her life was cut so short. I am prepared to accept that I will never accept it. *I don't even want to try.*

It still hurts me that she knew what was happening to her — that she had to deal with the emotional and physical pain all at once. But she was just so inspirational in her dying days. She was still trying to give advice, to protect us and to love us to the very end, despite how much she was suffering. *She was in so much pain — I can never take that away.* She constantly reminded us that she'd had such a wonderful life marrying Dad and bringing us three up. She would tell us that there were so many children with cancer, and that she felt lucky she had lived such a full, long life of laughter and good times. She was so graceful and so dignified about the fact that she was going to die. *How could anyone cope with such a thing?* She showed an inner strength I can't imagine I will ever have. She was so selfless and nothing short of incredible. If I turn out to be half the woman that she was, then I will be a very lucky lady. I will never forget her considerate words about others suffering more than her and she is right, of course — there are always people in worse situations than your own. I cannot comprehend what it must feel like for a parent to lose a child, nor a child far younger than me to lose a parent — but those people are now in my thoughts more than ever.

No lessons in school prepare you for the loss of a loved one. No books or websites that I have found can fully explain what you are going through. Grief is something that I do not believe you can ever completely define, explain or understand, whether you have lost someone or not. Every single person on this planet will deal with it in a completely different way: the definition is unique for us all. I know that in the case of my immediate family, we have grieved in very different ways and at completely different times — all of us would sometimes be too scared to share, in case we brought someone else down with us. For that reason, I have tried my hardest to deal with it on my own. I have become more used to it over time — it no longer scares me as much as it once did. I just use those dark moments to have a think and try to clear my head without burdening anyone else around me.

With such an individual take on things, it can result in a feeling of pure loneliness — regardless of how large the network of support that may surround you. The loneliness was something that I hadn't predicted at all — not with such a close family and large network of friends.

My mum did warn me about the mixture of feelings that I would experience. You see, she lost her mum at a similar age to me — her mum was only fifty-nine years old, too. She told me not to fight anything — told me not to beat myself up or hold anything in and just let everything out and not bottle it up. I still can't believe my mum was so selfless — still helping us in her last moments. My mum barely spoke about what happened with her own mum — she found it too difficult to talk about it. I got the sense that she was warning me not to go down that same route of silence and it is another reason to add to the growing list of motivations behind 60 Postcards.

You cannot possibly predict when you are going to be hit by grief. Nor can you predict the power with which it will strike. We are powerless. And I have heard this from so many people who have suffered a loss years before me. Unfortunately, the length of time since you have lost someone seems irrelevant.

Perhaps the strikes of emotional agony become less frequent, but it will just take one small thing — one short moment — to knock you off your feet again.

It was only a few months ago, on a training course with work, where a conversation about people taking time off due to the loss of a family member triggered an uncontrollable effect in me. It was a year and a half after Mum had died so I was feeling OK. *I've got this.* But my body didn't seem to agree. The shakes started, I felt like all of the blood had rushed out of me, my eyes were welling up and I felt sick to the stomach. The shock of last year's trauma hit me out of nowhere and sent me right back down to my lowest times — it took days for me to shake that off. Losing a loved one is something that we will never get over, but we learn to deal with it as best we can. Even though these uncontrollable storms of grief hit us out of nowhere, I have found that from experiencing them over time, despite knowing that they can come at any instant, you find a way to settle the storm and the clouds part a little more quickly each time. *It will get brighter — it has to.*

As a human race, we are pre-warned that death is inevitable. The one thing that we can all guarantee in life is that we will die. *Forgive me for stating the obvious.* My point is, why then is it still such a taboo subject? Why do people run so far away from talking about it? *It is so important.* We are all so happy to chat (tweet/Facebook/blog) about what we had for dinner or what we thought about the latest box office film, but we are trapped in a society where talking about the people we have lost seems unacceptable. I, for one, would like the opportunity to talk freely about the lady who brought me into the world, taught me everything that I know, is part of me and I am part of her. The only way that those we have lost can live on is through our memories and by talking about them; which is exactly why I embarked on my postcard project in the first place. As daunting as it may have been, I wanted to shout to the world as loudly as I could and leave an imprint of Mum's memory as far as I could spread it.

I have been amazed and overwhelmed by just how many people that I have come across, through writing my blog, who have also suffered from loss. From blog readers to people who I have worked with — there is constantly news of someone else's tragic situation. Some of these people I have never even met and others I had met only once or twice — and yet, by talking about my own experience, it opened up the floor for them to speak out. It is not normally the first thing that you would reveal about yourself to a stranger, so I am glad that this story has been and continues to be used as a platform. As difficult as it may be for me to hear so many sad tales, it will never get me down because I like the fact that people feel able to talk to me and that it helps them to share. *I hope that I keep hearing from people.*

I will always remember when a friend, Jo, shared with me the beautiful concept that those of us who have lost someone automatically join a secret society. That has stuck with me ever since. It is so true — the minute that I know someone else has been through a similar situation, I feel an instant connection with them. And it goes to show that, however lonely we feel, we really are not completely deserted. We have to stick together and help one another from our own experiences. Grief does not need to be shouldered alone — and that does not just mean with the ones closest to you. Everyone eventually joins the society — however much we never want to be a part of it. *This is the largest society in the world.*

Since my mother has gone, I have taken comfort in a beautiful realisation — there is so much that she passed down to me: my looks, my ways and my traits. I barely noticed these when she was here — I just couldn't see them at all. But now they are everywhere. I have often received mickey-taking about the way that I eat. Give me a sandwich or a burger and I like to use a knife and fork. *Weird, I know.* I have to make sure that my plate looks neat at all times so I take ages to get through dinner. *Definitely weird — I still know.* Everything has to be cut up well and I also need to eat certain things in order. *OK, OK, it admittedly sounds a little unusual. But, hey — it's what I do!* And now I like it when people pick up on it — they can tease me to their heart's content, because I got this habit from Mum. And, for that reason, I have no intention of changing it.

I didn't used to see a physical resemblance to either my mother or my father when I looked in the mirror. Now, with the assistance of old photographs, I really do see similarities with Mum. I will never forget the first time that I dyed my hair after her death. Just like Mum, I started to get grey hairs in my mid-twenties (*I have recently heard these referred to as 'stress highlights' which I much prefer*) and so, thankfully, us ladies have the option to cover our hair in a fresh colour, in a mission to maintain our youth. *I am still twenty-one years old (plus quite a few more).* I wrapped my hair up in a towel and got a fright when I looked into the mirror. I burst into floods of tears. I could see my mum staring back at me. But it wasn't long before seeing her in my reflection became something that I adore.

Sometimes I can even hear my mum when I hum along to a tune, or I think of her when I am writing a million lists. I often get neurotic about my sisters being OK, just like Mum used to do. It's amazing that even all of the way up to my late twenties (OK, very late) I didn't fully digest the fact that the person who brought me into the world had passed on so many of her qualities. I feel guilty for any teenage strop I may have had. I wouldn't be on this earth if it was not for her. Something that I used to say so frequently is, 'Oh, God — I'm turning into my mother.' Now, I proudly announce, 'Thank God I am turning into my mother.'

'You don't appreciate what you've got until it's gone' is a cliché so obvious but so true (well, yes — that is exactly what a cliché is!). I am very thankful for the especially strong mother and daughter bond that I had with her when she was alive and definitely more so now that it has been taken away from me. Still, I am proud to say that I don't regret a thing. I constantly told her how much I love her and she knew that I appreciated her so much. The only thing I wish now is that I could remind her over and over — I wish I could tell her how amazing she was. She was so unassuming, so unaware of just how great she was. She would never in a million years believe that she was worth writing a whole book about. I hope that she will be able to read this from wherever she is.

So as I think about my journey of grief and a life without Mum, I think about the good things that have happened alongside this — everything that has stemmed from the tribute that I did for her. When I embarked on the mission, I had no idea how much it would change my life.

The positives of 60 Postcards have been endless and they continue to multiply with every month that goes by. The first thing that I have been able to achieve from it is to finally unleash a side of me that has been desperate to get out for years. I was living in a creative bubble, so many plans and ideas, but no way of putting these into action. I had no real drive or motivation. That was until I used the energy from my grief to channel it and transfer it into something totally different. To turn it on its head, change it up and create a project that I will be able to treasure for the rest of my life.

I am doing something that I am passionate

about. I think it is safe to say that the older you get, the more afraid you are to take risks. You get settled and secure and begin to doubt that you will ever be able to do something bold, something new or something that will throw you in the deep end. Well, I now intend to do the opposite. As long as it isn't damaging to my health, I will throw myself into the deep end as much as possible. The worst thing that can happen is that I tread water for a while or swim to the side; the best thing that can happen is I will find myself swimming to a better life. I don't ever want to look back and think, 'what if'. I would rather look back and be glad that I gave something a good try. *Now I have said it, I have to do it!*

My postcard venture has been utterly amazing at providing me with a focus and something to distract my mind. Just like my dad said to me after Mum's funeral about getting back to work and keeping ourselves busy — this project has done that for me but with so many more benefits thrown in. It has kept me so busy that sometimes I am so engrossed in it my mind doesn't even have a chance to think of the pain.

As time has gone on I have appreciated more and more how difficult it must be for friends during tragic times. I find that it is so often the case that *I* don't even know what I want from people, so how are my friends supposed to know? Some days I want people to ask if I am OK — some days I don't. Some days I am desperate to talk about Mum every minute of the day and some days I can't. Some days I simply want to run away. I am very lucky to have the friends that I have for being patient about this. They have been there more than I could ever have wished for.

Through this project I have not only heard from friends from the present but it has put me in touch with people from my past, as well. I lost touch with one of my best friends from university after I lost my phone and all my contacts and found that she was no longer on Facebook. I often thought about her and wondered if I would ever be able to find her again. And then in July, after I had just written my post named 'Serendipity' something amazing happened . . .

'Serendipity indeed! I have stumbled upon your blog Rachael Chadwick — (YOUR blog — amazing!) quite by accident. A happy accident! I'm not even sure I could remember why or how, all I know is I was on the train where I soon found myself a big teary and dribbly mess! I do also know that, whilst we don't see each other much (ever!) you were a huge part of my life and that means that I'm allowed to say that I am so incredibly proud of you and everything that you are doing!

I will raise a glass this evening to the wonderful Mummy Chadwick!

Love you long time lady,

Vixter xxx'

Wow! She found my blog by chance and we have been in touch ever since. I am so grateful that this is bringing so many people back into my world.

My family are so supportive in everything that I do and, most recently, of what I am doing with the 60 Postcards project. I was very worried on several occasions that this would dig up old feelings for them — I was conscious of the fact that, by telling my story, I was telling part of theirs as well. But this reminds me of something my dad said — it would be so interesting to see this written from his and my sisters' points of view. You would have four completely different versions of events — with different opinions, views and approaches to grief, not to mention a very different angle to that traumatic two weeks and two days. But they have been so excited to enjoy 60 Postcards with me — sharing my blog with friends and family, helping me to remember events from the past. I feel like this project has brought me even closer to them, as it has given us all an opportunity to talk about Mum so much more. One of my favourite parts of this whole experience has been hearing stories about Mum that I didn't even know before. She may be gone but I am still getting to know her and I plan to learn more about her with every year of my life.

I still cannot believe that all of those postcard finders picked up my handwritten note and got in touch with me. The rush of excitement that I felt with each response was so surprising, magical and uplifting all at once. It was the most on top of the world that I had felt in that dark year and it will be a feeling that will stay with me forever. I took a chance on people and they took a chance on me. This is humanity at its best.

I have been so pleased that the authenticity of handwritten words can be so far reaching. This may have all started in Paris but it has ended up reaching around the globe, as the finders return to their homes, all the way from Sheffield to New York, and from Texas to Spain. I feel like I have made new friends and, as I plan to continue a life where travel will play a huge part, I now have a growing number of familiar faces to visit on my explorations. I cannot wait to meet all my postcard finders and I truly hope that I continue to be in touch with them and involve them in all the news that 60 Postcards may bring in the future. The more amazing people I meet through this journey, the more inspired I am to push forward. I never intended for this to be a social experiment but I guess, in a way, that's what it has become — and what a wonderful one it has turned out to be (*she says, as she plots more ideas*).

★ ★ ★

My mum simply loved being a mum. She wasn't just a mother figure to us — she became one to so many others, too, as so many family friends have reminded me (even recently) that they often thought of my mum as a mentor. On top of this, she was incredibly passionate about education and her job as a teacher. That is why I am thrilled that her school got in touch through the letters — to be receiving such mature support from such young people was so moving. And if children are encouraged to be able to talk freely about loss, then maybe there will be some hope for the future and the taboo of talking about death may be slowly dissolved. *I plan to help it dissolve in any way that I can.* Those letters are a gift that I can always keep and my mum would be so proud of those children for the beautiful words that they wrote.

My dad was invited to Allenbourn Middle School in the summer to attend the opening of a new garden that was created in memory of Mum. Some of the children were there and read out their letters in front of a crowd of people. One of the students got in touch with me to tell me about it and said that she hadn't had a chance to say goodbye to my mum so she hoped that she was making up for it by reading her letter on that day. What a lovely thought. In the middle of the garden there is a bench with a message on it, which reads, 'Live Life to the Full' — it is absolutely perfect. Mum always encouraged us to live by that mantra. As we have learnt the hard way, life really is too short.

The next time I heard from the school, they were doing a project of their own called Team Assist, which mirrored the task of 60 Postcards, and they left messages about my mum in places around the UK. I was ecstatic to hear that they had received their own responses and I hope that this is not the first time that my project is tried out by other people. *I want to start a postcard revolution!*

Getting children involved was something that I got to experience for a second time when Paris Crew member Clare invited me into her school to do a talk. Clare was hosting a day to inspire the children to think about their experiences in the wider world with a focus on work/life balance and doing things that you are passionate about. I was honoured to be involved and I absolutely adored being a part of it. It was actually a huge step for me (luckily it hadn't even crossed my mind until I was there), but it would be the first time that I would stand up in front of a large group in public and say the words, 'My mum died last year.' I really enjoyed telling them my postcard tales and I decided to bring along some postcards (naturally) for the students to write their own messages about an achievement, an inspiration or a goal for the future. As I wandered around the room, they were asking questions, buzzing with ideas and it was a real insight into why my mum loved teaching so much.

One thing that I have really appreciated about sharing my story is being given the opportunity for my voice to be heard. A written voice which is, I have been told, very similar to the speaking version. If you read this, essentially you are getting to know me — nice to meet you! I feel overwhelmingly honoured — truly (madly, deeply) honoured — that through the power of words, I can express the power of loss. But, more than that, I have the opportunity to talk about the fact that if you attack grief from a different angle, it can create the most incredible experiences, stories and new friendships along the way.

My personality has most definitely changed over the past year and a half. They say, 'What doesn't kill you makes you stronger' and I completely agree with that. I am more decisive now and, even though I don't know where I will end up, I am not afraid to change direction if it means I may find the right path. I now find myself more fearless than fearful. I am no longer afraid of anything — not even death. I have learnt, in the harshest way possible, never to believe that you are invincible. I was so naive — I didn't think anything bad could happen to me. But now, after watching my mother die, I know that nothing can be worse than that. I should be able to get through anything and I have to use this newfound strength to my advantage.

And just when I thought that I had heard the last from a postcard finder, I was at a wedding of my friends Aaron and Kerry on 19th October, 2013, just two days after my return from Paris, when I received a surprise email:

Hi,
I found this beautiful postcard on the padlock bridge in Paris on Monday. I was

literally moved to tears when I read it, much to my daughter's amusement.

It's such a wonderful way to pay tribute to your mum. I wish you much love and happiness on your journey through Paris and through life.

Suzanne x

I couldn't reply quickly enough:

Good morning Suzanne,

Thank you so much for the lovely email! I burst into tears as I read it. It was so nice of you to get in touch :)

I am not sure if you have had a chance to look at the blog, it has been utterly bonkers. I scattered some postcards, got some responses and started a blog. I feel overwhelmed and honoured that I am able to leave such a tribute for mum.

Please may you tell me a little about yourself? What you were doing in Paris etc?

Obviously, I completely understand if this is not possible. Your message is enough! It really has made my week.

Much love (and hi to the daughter who now thinks you've lost it!)

Rachael xx

Hi Rachael,

Let me just say as a mother of two (sometimes ;)) wonderful girls, I can't think of any better tribute to your mum. I have hopefully instilled in my girls the importance of spreading your wings far and wide, the scarier the better. No matter what they encounter good, bad or downright ugly, I'll always be here to put them back on track. I hope I'm right in saying that I think that's where you are coming from and I think it's marvellous you have the courage to do this. I read a little of your blog last night and thoroughly enjoyed it. I'm hoping to get stuck into it when I have time to sit and read it with a cuppa.

I have spent the last few months coming back and forward from Glasgow to Paris trying to find an apartment for my 19-year-old daughter who is studying at Nanterre until January. I was in Paris last Sunday until Wednesday visiting her with my husband and my 13-year-old, Mia, who thought I was a blubbering idiot! My oldest Hollie would have been crying along with me at your postcard! Love Lock Bridge certainly put the romance back in Paris for me :)

Good luck and I will be looking out for the published masterpiece at my local book store!

Much love
Suzanne x

There is so much that I love about these messages from Suzanne. For one, the unexpectedness that my postcard was even read by anyone at all — I really thought that one was gone forever. But the fact that it was found by a mother to girls means just so much. I know, in my heart, that my mum would echo everything that Suzanne says about her girls. It was almost as if Mum was talking to me through that message.

As I write this, my 30th birthday approaches and I find myself reflecting over the past year and a half and acknowledge just how much has changed. This is a milestone birthday that so many people dread — the new chapter of the thirties can seem a little daunting in an I-should-be-an-adult-by-now way. But, even though my mum may not be able to make it to my birthday celebrations, I know that I have the best gift that a girl could wish for — I am leaving a long-lasting memory for my beautiful mum.

I cannot wait to see all of my family and friends, and to raise a glass to the lady who cannot be there. I will have most of the Paris Crew with me. They have been busy with work and play and on travelling adventures of their own — Katie is flying back from Brazil where she is living while she enjoys a two-year secondment from work. The only person that will be missing from the party will be Beth. But she can be forgiven for her absence because she needs to rest and relax, as I am delighted to say that she is going to have a baby — our first Paris Crew member to become a mother. She is due three days after Mother's Day and I couldn't be more excited to meet the little one.

The journey of this project, blog and now book has really made it hit home just how much we do things to make our family proud. Everything I do is for them. There is absolutely nothing in this world like a mum's pride, though. Of course, people often think that you need your mum in the bad times, but I fear the achievements and the good times ahead, too. It will always be painful — she should be here to share them with me.

Over the past 20 months since her death, I have been thinking of how I am going to cope without her in the future. Anything at all that would help. My dad has coined the phrase, 'What would Viv do?' Over the years my mum shared so many words of comfort and wisdom, I now try to think about what she would say in response to me. I think when we ask our mums for advice, we probably already know what they are going to say — it is the reassurance that we are after — knowing that we are doing the right thing.

I also find myself thinking back to when I was little — you know when you were so excited to be performing in a school play or concert? You would be waiting for it to begin, sat in the wings, scouring the audience desperately, just to see your mum. You wanted to see her smiling face, a thumbs up, a nod or a wink — reassuring you that you *can* do it and that she is right there watching and supporting you. I feel like when things go well or when I want her to see something, I will forever be looking out into that audience searching for her. But I just have to imagine that she is there. I tell myself that I just haven't been able to spot her in the crowded room. The show must go on.

Oh the show will most definitely go on! The most beautiful thing about 60 Postcards is that it will now be a part of my life forever and the unpredictability of where it will lead me next is so exciting — I have absolutely no idea, but it is almost a given that it will include a lot of magic, a spice of adventure and the addition of many more new friends, whether near or far. My mum was and continues to be the centre of my universe and I feel as though 60 Postcards has become the bright shining star in my life that has brought me closer to her, even though she is no longer with me.

*   *   *

When I wrote about the tragic time in which my mum died, I mentioned the unwritten family rule — to try our best not to break down in front of Mum and to try our best not to mention the future. Although I did try my very best in those traumatic sixteen days, I was unable to keep to it completely. I broke the rule — something I am not proud of at all.

It was just a few nights before Mum passed away and all of the family were together in the lounge — one of the many times that we were trying so hard to watch the TV and not her. Staring at her, worrying with every breath that she took that it may be her last. Mum was too tired to stay up any longer that evening and so I offered to take her up to bed. I helped her up the stairs, a task that took so long. Her body was now so weak that she was clearly trying to use every single bit of energy that she had left to climb to the top. Even at this point I was fighting with all of my might not to crumble in front of her. These were the very same stairs in our family home that she had been dashing up and down for years, even just weeks ago. My poor mum was fading away in front of my eyes at a speed I couldn't keep up with. And there was absolutely nothing that I could do about it.

As she got into bed, I decided that I would stay with her for a while. I wanted to be with her. I lay in bed, holding her hand and it was at that moment I realised this may be my only chance. I couldn't stop myself — I had to say *something*. I was struggling to get my words out, tears streaming down my face — before I knew it I was sobbing uncontrollably. I declared to Mum that I didn't want to do this — this life — without her.

I asked her if there was any way that she could write me a letter. One that she could write herself so that I could tell people about her and in case I ever have children in the future. For the children that she was never going to get the chance to meet or be the most incredible granny to; a role I know she was born to do and would have loved so much. She began to cry with me as we acknowledged, out loud, for the first and final time that we were going to lose each other forever. She shook her head and told me that both physically and emotionally there was no way that she could write that letter. Guilt rushed over me as she whispered, 'I'm sorry.'

What had I done? Why was I putting my mum through this? I hadn't meant to upset her and I wished I could take it back. I told her that I understood why she couldn't do it. Except, deep down, I was desperately hoping that she would change her mind. She didn't, she couldn't.

What followed was something that will stay with me forever. My mum looked at me, squeezed my hand and told me that she completely trusted my way with words — that I had been given a gift and that I could tell people about her in that way.

I don't think she ever expected it would be in a book.

Some scatter ashes — I am scattering words.

Vivienne Chadwick née Love — this is your gift, your tribute and your legacy.

I love you.

★   ★   ★

Now, take the postcard that you used as a bookmark and write a message on it. Write about someone who inspires you, whether they are still with us or not.

Keep it, share it or perhaps even leave it somewhere for someone else to find.

Welcome to Team 60 Postcards.

Acknowledgements

I feel like there are a million and one people to thank for guiding and supporting me through the journey of writing this book. Of course, I cannot possibly mention every single one of you, so I would like to offer my thanks to a special few . . .

My family

Dad — You are my hero — you always have been and you always will be. Sarah and Hannah, my gorgeous sisters — You are my best friends and I will be right by your side forever. I know that this has been an emotional tale to tell — chapters of this book have been the chapters of our lives and I can only hope that my tribute for Mum will continue to create magical memories for us all for many years to come — we are in this together. I may have written thousands of words in this book, but I will never be able to find enough to tell you just how much I love you.

Joe — Thank you for being the best husband to Hannah that I could wish for.

And I am so grateful for you being there for all of us in our hours, months and years of need.

Mum's Family

To the 'Loves' — Brothers Geoff, Steve and Graham and their families and to Nicola, Amber and Lucy — I know we will all miss her every single day, but I hope that this book is as much a gift and a celebration of her life for you as it is for me.

My Agent

Jo — Thank you for showing me the way. Ever since I first met you, I knew that we would become good friends and I am so glad that is what we have become.

The Publishers

A huge thanks to everyone at Simon & Schuster (including Mike, Rik, Anneka, Richard and Helen) for helping me to share my story and understanding how much it means to me. In particular to . . .

Briony — You took a chance on me and made me believe that I could do this — I will be forever grateful.

Jo W — Thank you for everything. You have been so wonderful to work with and I really appreciate your guidance through my 'first-book worries'!

'Swanage Jo' — Not only did you unleash your editing wizardry on this book, but you were also there for me when my emotions were taking over — you picked me up when I was down and it means the world to me.

The 60 Postcards Crew

You not only helped me to celebrate my mother's 60th birthday, but also to launch a project, which has changed my whole life. I will never forget (pun still intended).

My Postcard Finders

Had you not picked up that handwritten note and got in touch with me, I am certain that this story would never have been told. I feel honoured that you are part of Team 60 Postcards and I am looking forward to meeting you all one day.

Blog Readers

Your messages, emails and tweets of support have been comforting, encouraging and an absolute privilege to receive. Your loyalty in returning to my blog each week has given me a reason to carry on.

My Mugger

To the gentleman who stole my laptop two weeks before my first-draft deadline — thank you for reminding me that the little things in life just don't matter. (And thanks, Mum, for teaching me always to back up my work!)

Luke — You saved the day by lending me your laptop to complete this book — thank you so much.

My Rocks

Caroline — You have been there every single step of the way. I hope that we are sat sipping wine in Café Boheme — putting the world to rights — when we are seventy years old and more.

Marcus — Thank you for being on call every day and night and for so many walks to help me clear my head, when at times I wasn't sure it would clear at all.

Beccy — From dancing with me in the kitchen, to shouting words of encouragement as I typed away like a crazy person, you have been the most wonderful friend I could wish for.

To ALL of my friends and family, mentioned in this book or not. Your support through the bad times and the good has been simply incredible. I will always be there for you too — please remember that.

And finally I would like to thank my inspiration — my mother — Vivienne Chadwick (née Love). You will always be in my head, in my heart, my voice and now this book. I will never stop trying to make you proud.

The show must go on — for you.

We do hope that you have enjoyed reading this large print book.

Did you know that all of our titles are available for purchase?

We publish a wide range of high quality large print books including:
Romances, Mysteries, Classics
General Fiction
Non Fiction and Westerns

Special interest titles available in large print are:
The Little Oxford Dictionary
Music Book
Song Book
Hymn Book
Service Book

Also available from us courtesy of Oxford University Press:
Young Readers' Dictionary
(large print edition)
Young Readers' Thesaurus
(large print edition)

For further information or a free brochure, please contact us at:
Ulverscroft Large Print Books Ltd.,
The Green, Bradgate Road, Anstey,
Leicester, LE7 7FU, England.
Tel: (00 44) 0116 236 4325
Fax: (00 44) 0116 234 0205